To Ann & Nick
Benedict, Francesca & Thea.
with wishes that we will welcome [illegible] Jersey
Fondest love
Elaine & [illegible] Dec 2002.

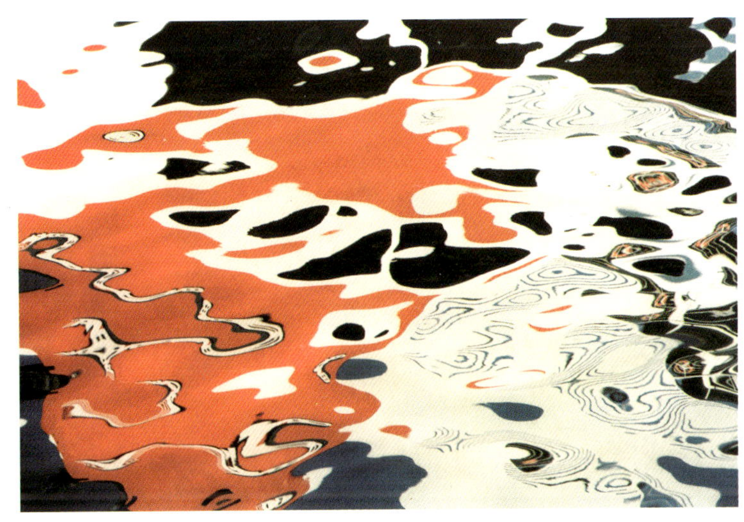

Focussed on Jersey

Published by
Brian Skelley Photography
Le Jardin de la Fontaine
La Valleé des Vaux
St Helier, Jersey

In association with

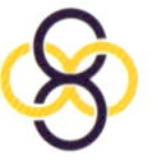

Channel Island Features Limited
P.O. Box 133, Jersey, Channel Islands

ISBN: 0-9544054-0-4

I first met Brian when he was a student at Hautlieu many years ago, where I taught Art, then later at the excellent Portofino Restaurant in St. Aubins. I became increasingly aware that the many photographs that lined the walls there, and most recently of course, at the Borsalino Rocque in Grouville, were not the work of an ordinary photographer. Here was the person with an artist's eye, with a passionate response and an ability to select the essential elements of a composition and present them in a powerful manner. I was most impressed. These feelings were more fully confirmed when I saw an exhibition of Brian's photographs and obtained a copy of his book developed in association with Jack Clarke's poetry, 'Jersey Remembered'.

As a result of this, when Brian told me about the book he is producing now and asked me if I would write the foreword, I unhesitatingly agreed and considered the request a great privilege. Later in the week when I went to his house to look through some of the material and discuss it with him it was clear that the whole idea meant so very much to him.

For those who know Brian, and there are many, he has an overwhelming enthusiasm when he hits upon an idea and needs to share his feelings with others. Such an idea, and a particularly good one, is the book of his photographs to be accompanied by associated poems written by students from Jersey.

Standing in front of the various classes with selections of photographs, talking about them and posing so many questions as to their possible interpretations, he builds up a bond with his young audiences. They then attempt to translate their feelings of the images seen into their own words and their own poems, and because of this bond their responses are both whole-hearted and genuine. Brian said that reading through some of the poems that they had written had at times reduced him to tears.

As I looked through more of the work, my enthusiasm and total support of Brian's idea became apparent. Here was an opportunity for the students not only to participate in what will become an important Island project, but also to develop their creative processes and to be rewarded by seeing their poems printed in a beautifully produced book.

I am also sure that the thrill of discovering that they, the students, possess possibly unexpected levels of creativity, will be a kick start to the furtherance of their skills in the future and I would not be at all surprised if the wonderful idea of this book leads to similar ventures with other students years from Island schools.

Derek Crow

October 14th 2002

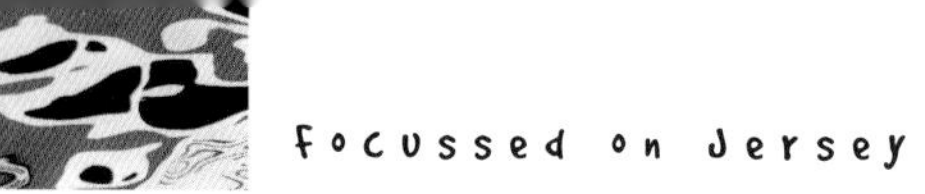

There is an old saying that "the people do not make the land, it is the land that makes the people", and without question, the forces of nature have had a profound effect on Jersey and its people, the reality of the Island is truly captivating - despite its small size, there is a variety of landscape which is only matched by the ever changing moods of sky and sea.

This book combines stunning visual images with the vibrant imagery of poetry written by pupils from many of the Island's schools. I am sure that it will bring endless pleasure to many.

Tom McKeon

Director of Education

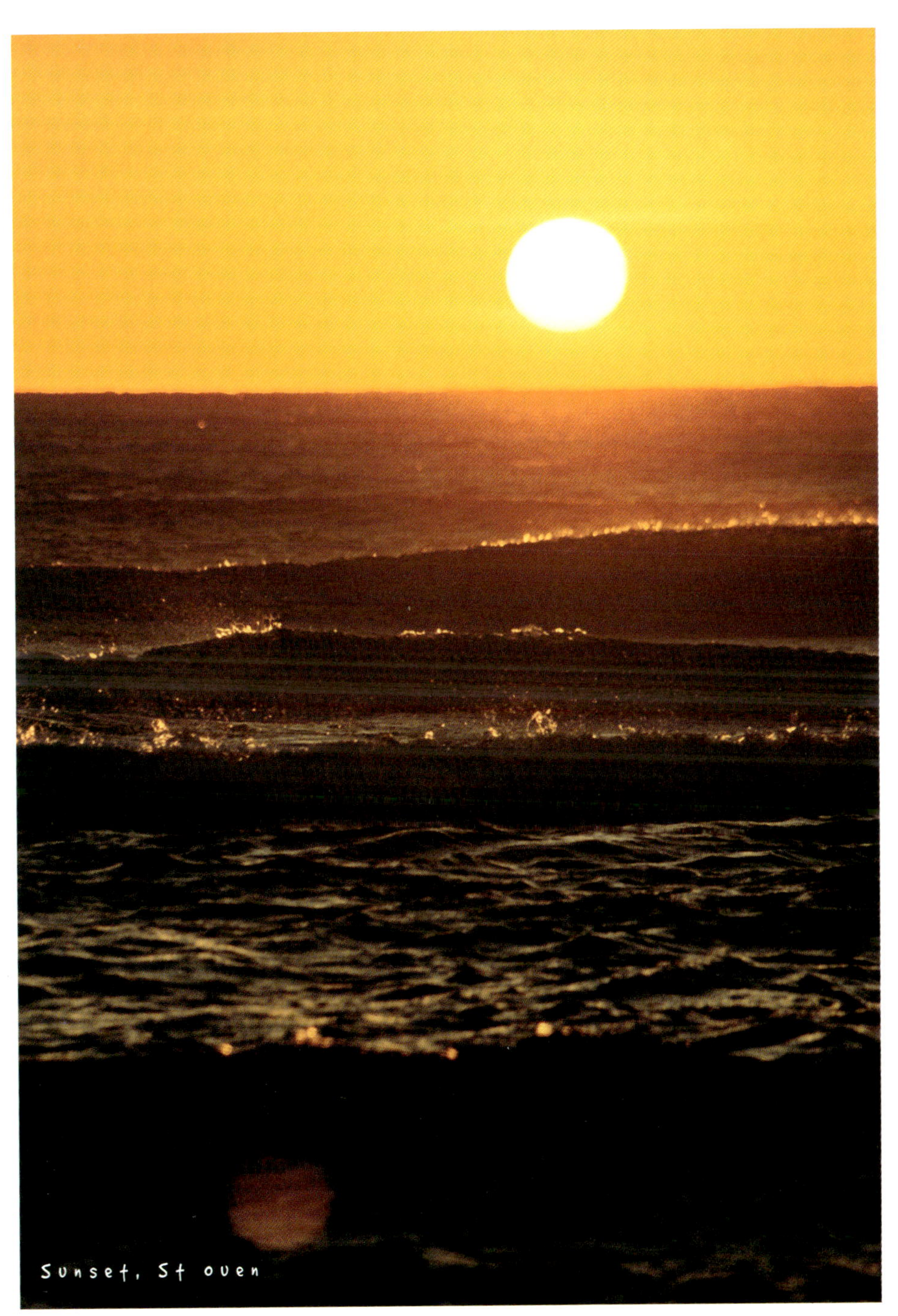

Sunset, St Ouen

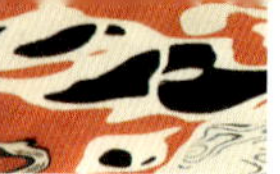

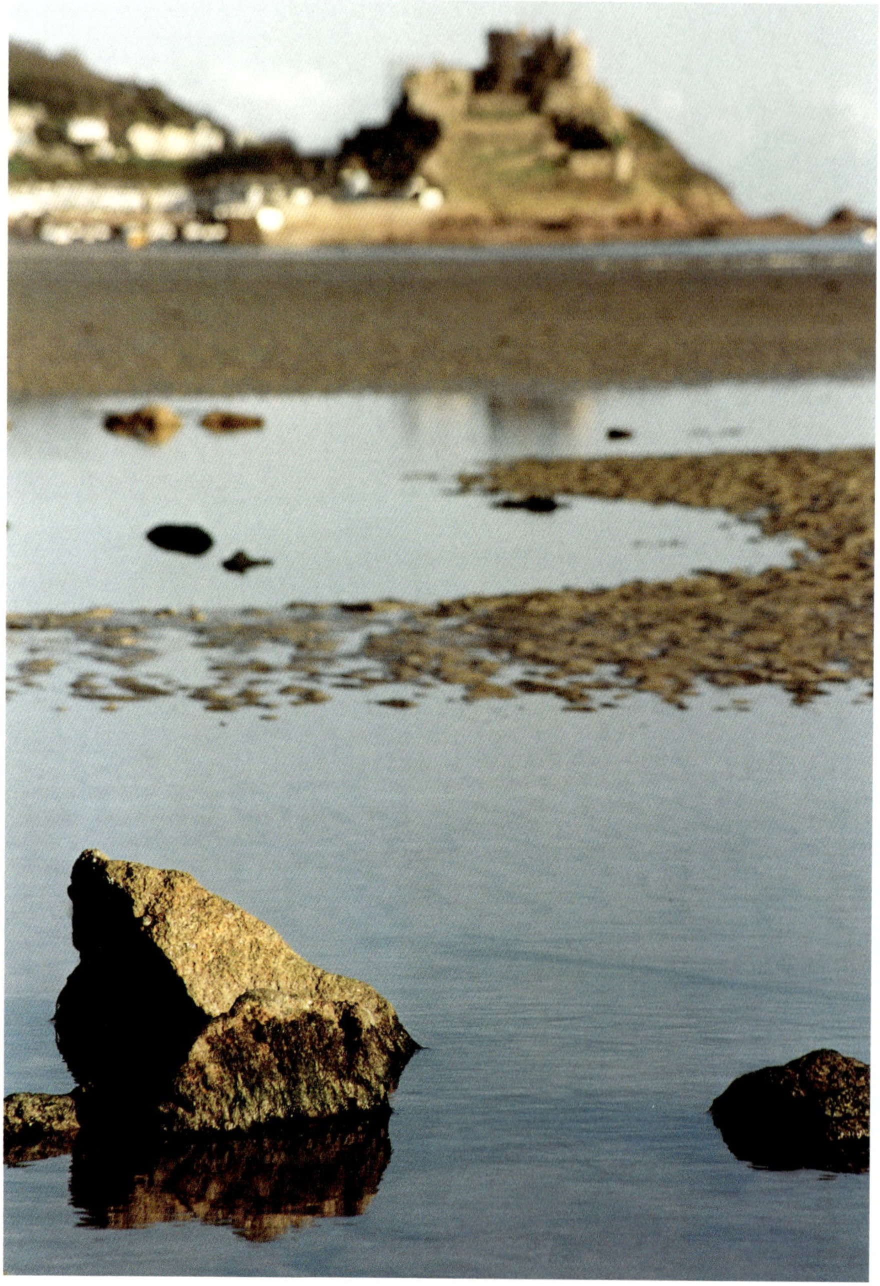

The Rock of Gorey

The Rock of Gorey

By Seth Crosby

Le Rocquier

I am just a lonely rock,
Around me a lake of salt,
But soon I'll be up high in the sky,
All gleaming without fault

I will be in the castle yonder,
Fair maidens I will save,
Arrows, armour and clash of sword,
The dragon I will brave.

I wonder what things I'll face,
Unruly wind and rain,
But I will keep brave knight dry,
And drive the rain to drain.

For I am just a lonely rock,
Around me a lake of salt,
But soon I'll be up high in the sky,
All gleaming without fault.

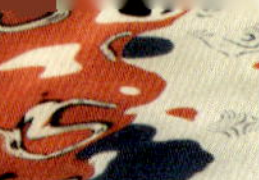

Jersey, a place of freedom

By Simon Anger and David Queen
Haute Valleé

Jersey is a place of freedom
Jersey is the place to be
Jersey has the sand and the sea
People don't appreciate being free.
Tourists go to the statue
To see what it means to be free
Once they have seen it
They will feel like you and me.
When the Germans came
They stopped us being free
But Jersey did not fight
Because Jersey is a peaceful place
For you and me.
But now Jersey is a place of freedom
Jersey is the place to be
Let's keep Jersey free
It should be kept like this
For you and me.

Untitled

By Dan Lezala
Les Quennevais

I wasn't there
But I can imagine
The feeling that they got.
After years of imprisonment,
Hitler just couldn't win.
The community,
The society,
The brotherhood of the island,
Finally they can say they're free.
Free from fear,
Free from the intensity,
Free from the thought of death.
A moment captured in bronze.
The expressions on their faces,
They will never change,
But, they will never be the same.

Liberation
Square

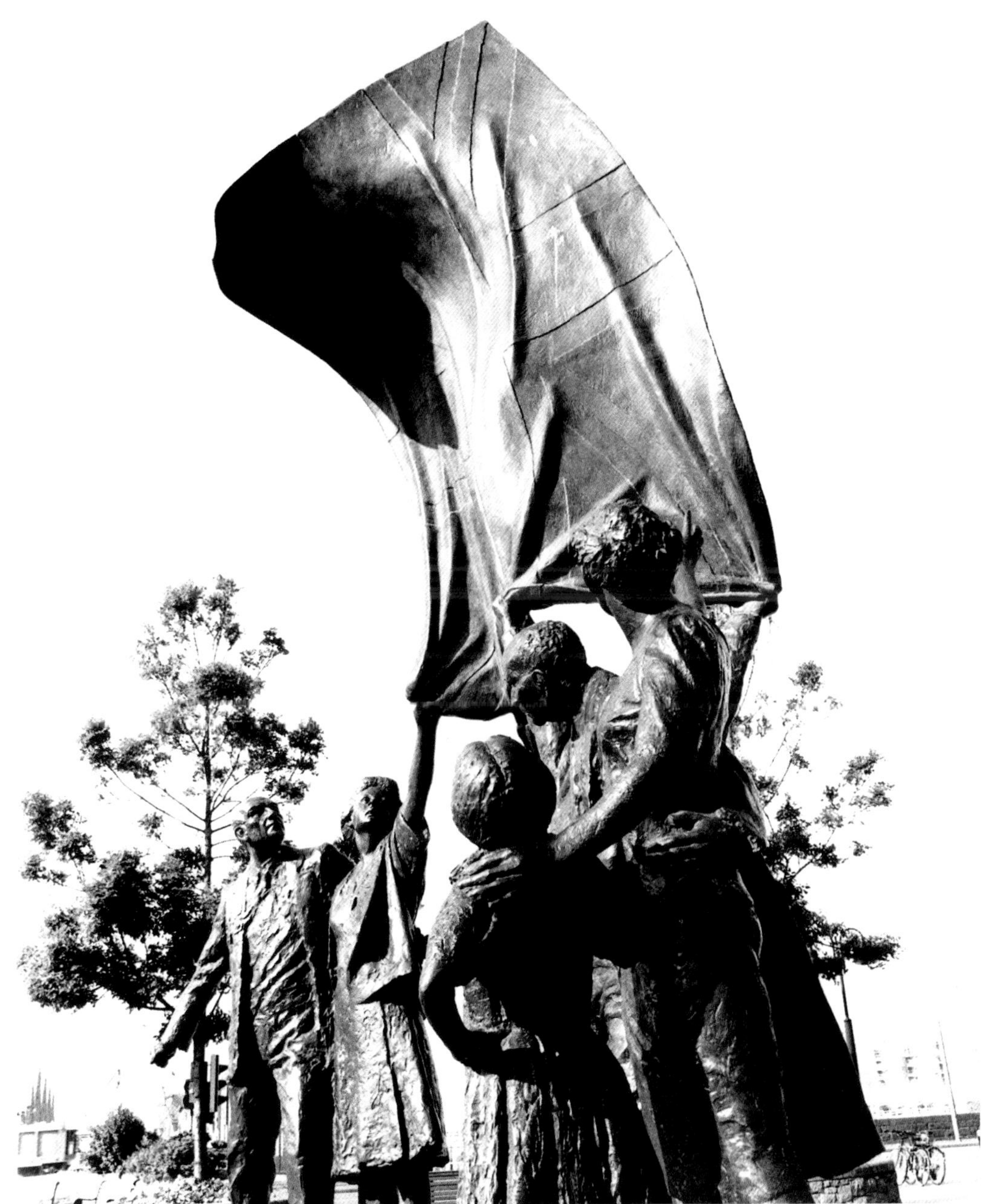

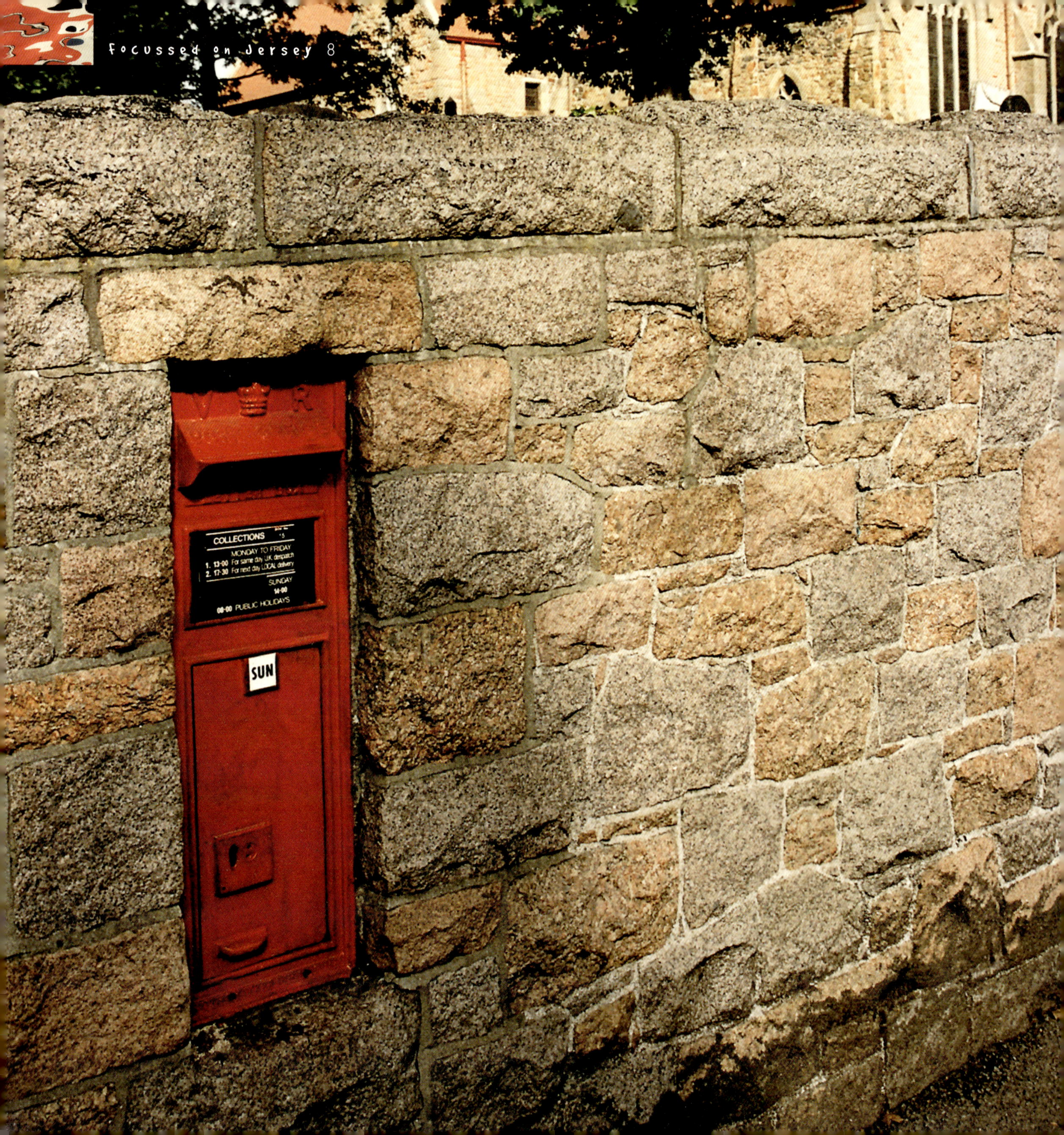
V R
COLLECTIONS
MONDAY TO FRIDAY
1. 13-00 For same day U.K. despatch
2. 17-30 For next day LOCAL delivery
SUNDAY
14-00
00-00 PUBLIC HOLIDAYS
SUN

Postbox

By Christopher Lawrence

De La Salle

It goes through the slot,
Paper and pen.
Monday to Friday,
Collections at ten.
The postman comes round, he rides on his bike,
He'll take letters or parcels, whatever you like.
As long as there are stamps,
Which you have to buy,
And an address that's correct
Or he won't comply.
It's the postbox, metal and red,
It's too old and slow so I'll E-mail instead.

Post Box, St Saviour's Church

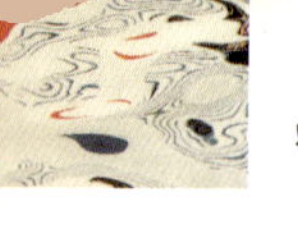

Waddling Home

By Kieran Carré
Grainville

The winter has come again,
The people have all gone home.
Nothing is left on the beach,
We are here alone.
So let's waddle on home.

It is getting dark now,
It is very cold and wet.
The water is rising slowly,
The sun will soon set.
So let's waddle on home.

The winter is going to be tough,
But we're sure we will pull through.
We need to store food, more than enough,
For us the harsh winter is nothing new.
So let's waddle on home.

The summer will come again next year,
The beach will be filled once more.
But for now let's dream about next year,
As we stroll along the shore.
So let's waddle on home.

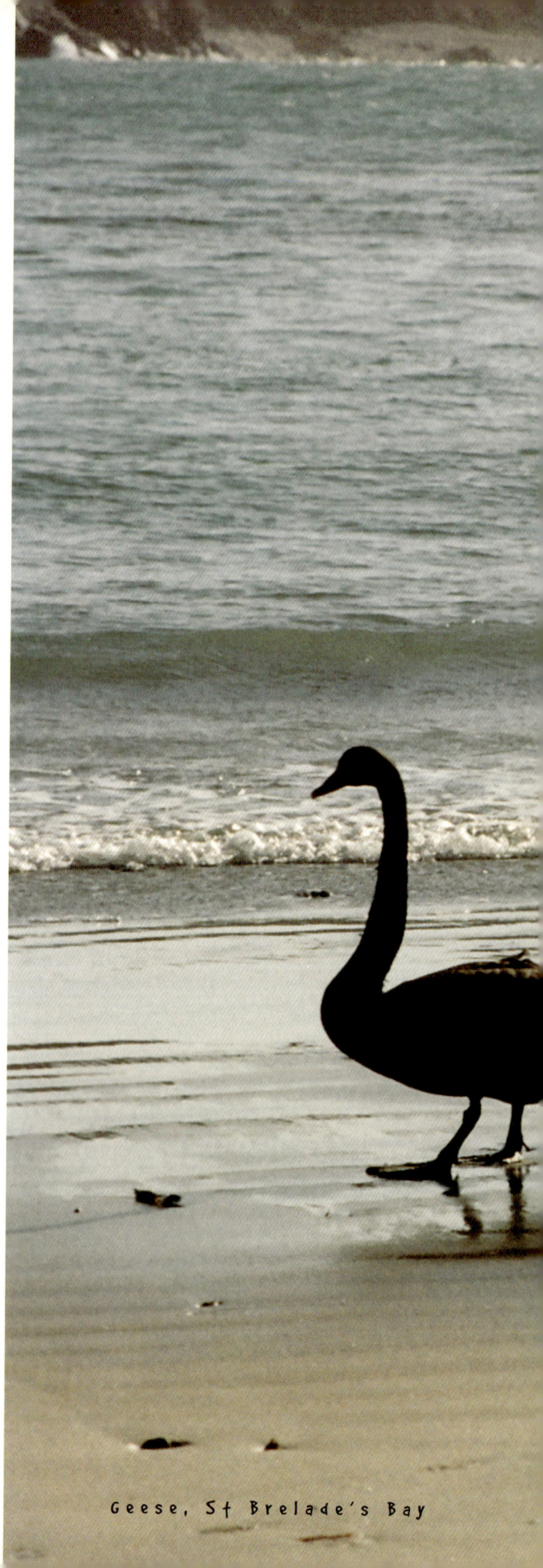

Geese, St Brelade's Bay

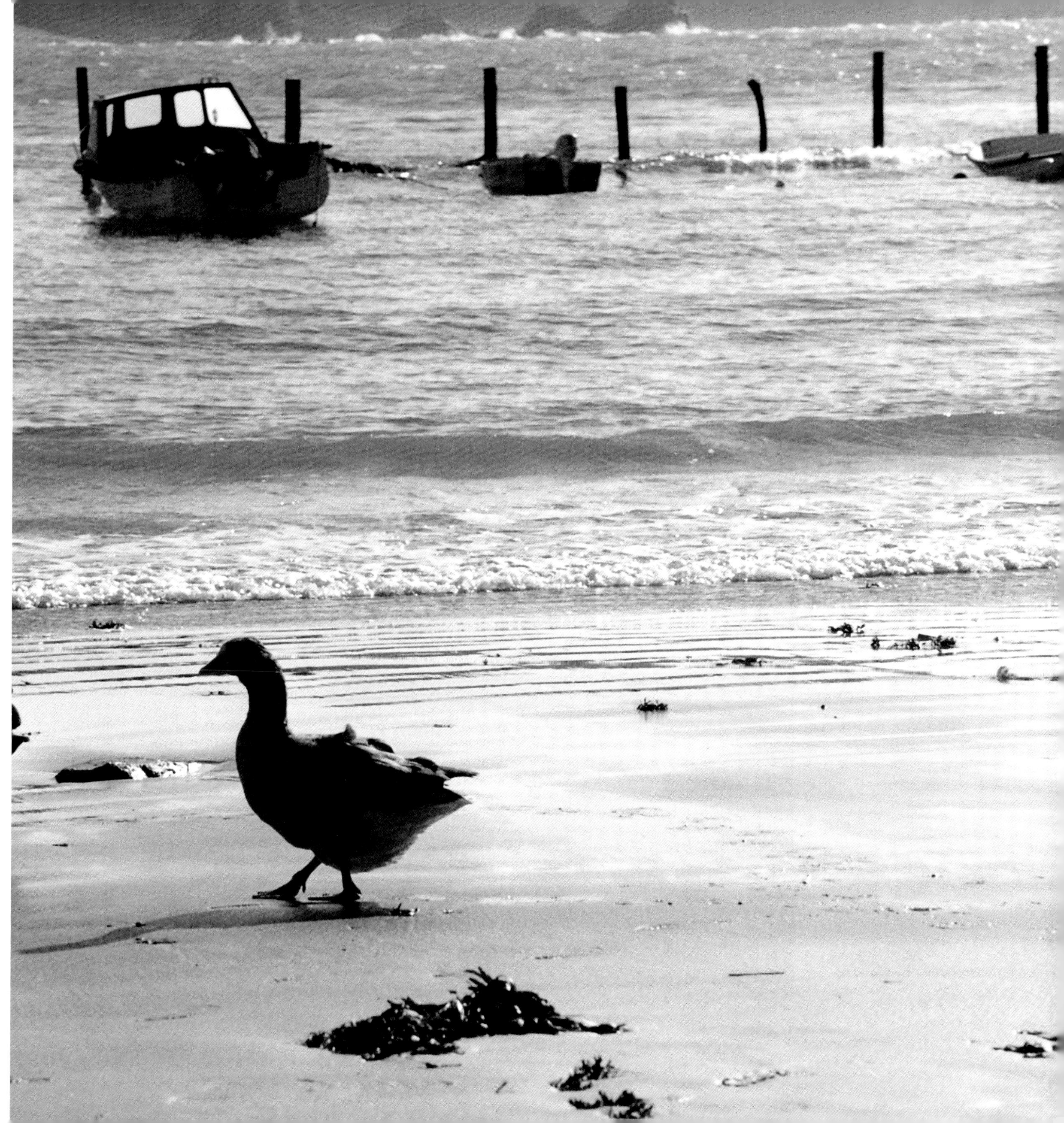

Footprints in the sand

By Andrea Roberts
Jersey College for Girls

The tide turns, oh so very quickly
Covering the day's spectacular works.
Gone are the castles, the tunnels and the holes
So carefully constructed by young and young at heart.
Gone also are tomorrow's would be architects, builders, writers and more.

For a short time only the canvas is well concealed.
But, then, yet again, so very quickly,
The tide goes on it s outward journey once more
Leaving behind it a saggy canvas
With decorations in different shapes and sizes.

As the canvas dries, it glistens and gleams
Perfectly smooth but for a short time only.
A lone walker takes an early stroll
The canvas is used yet again.
This time, by footprints in the sand.

Janvrin's Tomb

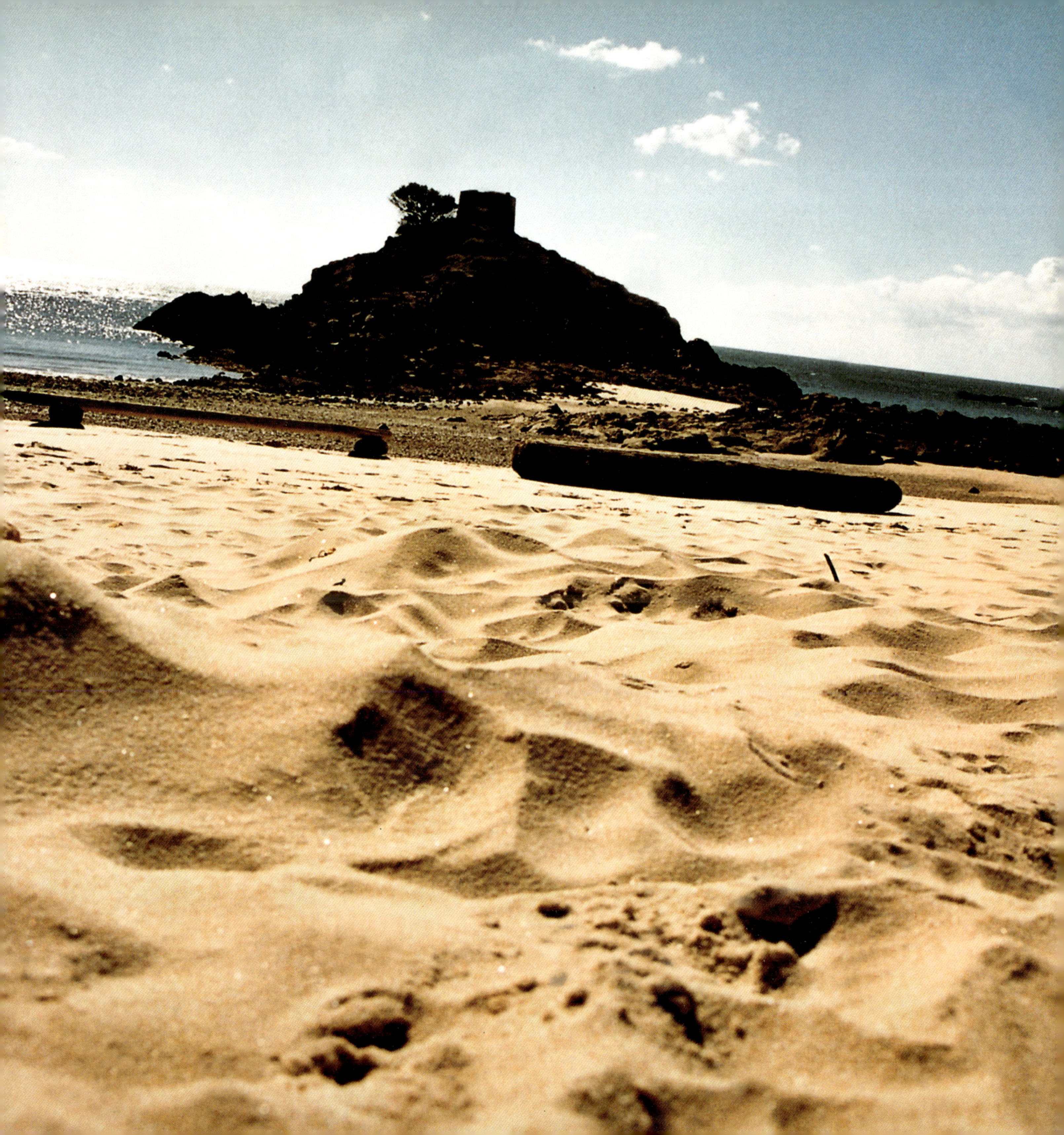

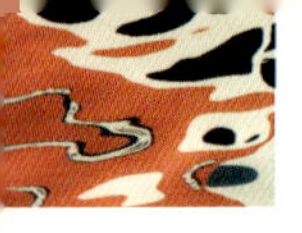

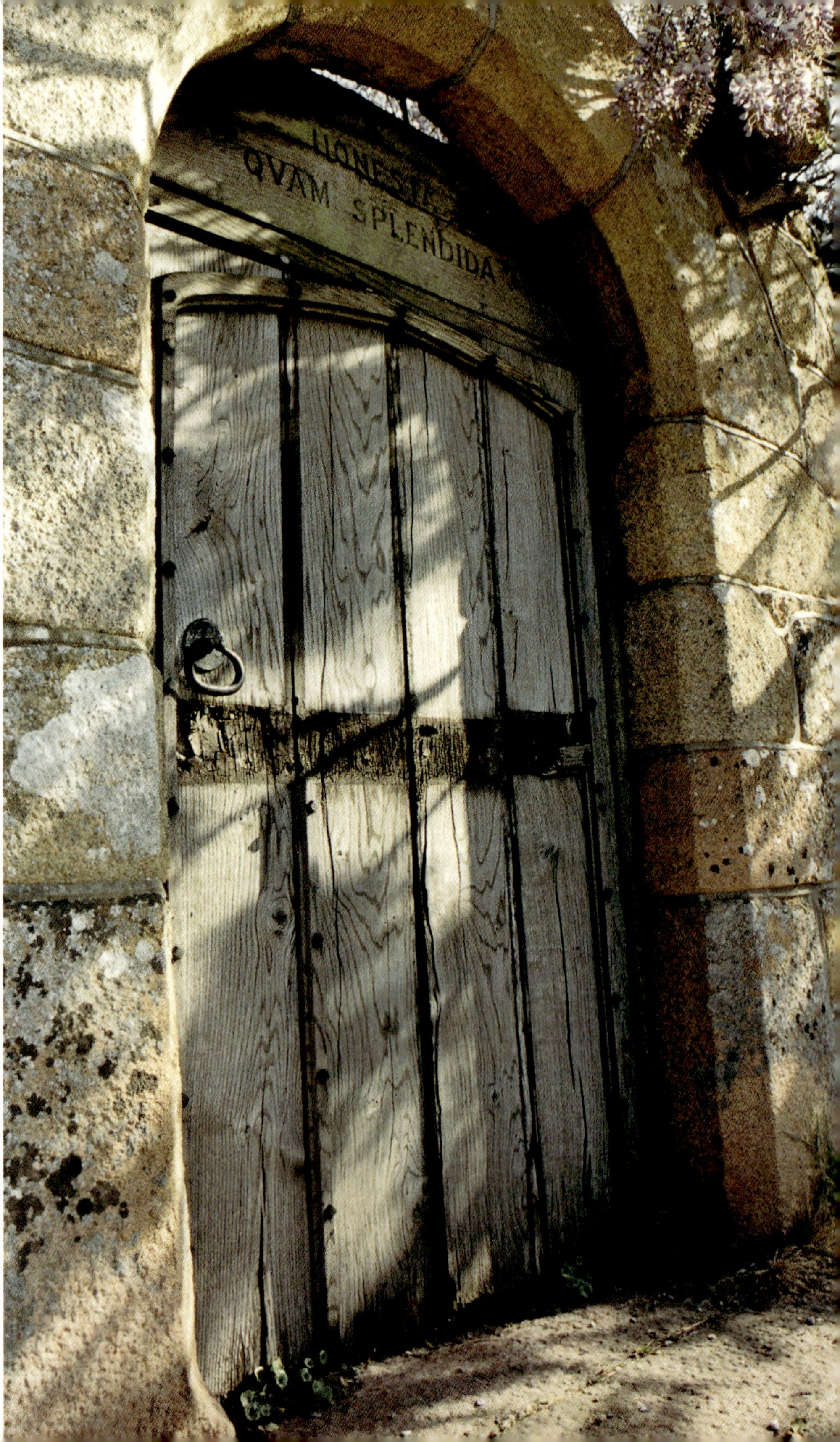

Uonesia Qvam Splendida

Honesty How Splendid, Trinity

The Gate

By Julian Birch
Victoria College

I am the gate
so solid of oak,
I am the gate
with hinges best poke,
I am the gate
with secrets to hide,
I am the gate
that invites you inside.

I am the gate
with a welcoming jar,
I am the gate
with a forbidding bar,
I am the gate
that opens when bright,
I am the gate
that closes at night.
I am the gate
that will be locked,
I am the gate
that will not be blocked,
I am the gate.

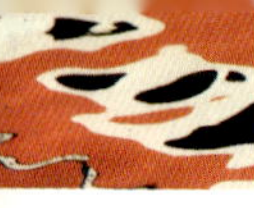

Untitled

By Laura Cuddon-Large
Beaulieu

The glistening sun on the waves,
The faint rocks out to sea,
The misty clouds in the sky,
This is how the beach is for me.

People love to go to the beach,
Some go there everyday
To paddle in the sea
In Jersey's radiant bay.

In summer the beach is crowded
With all the people enjoying the sun
In winter the sea is busy,
With all the surfers having fun.

People in Jersey are lucky
To live near the stunning sea
I wouldn't like to live anywhere else
But here where we are free.

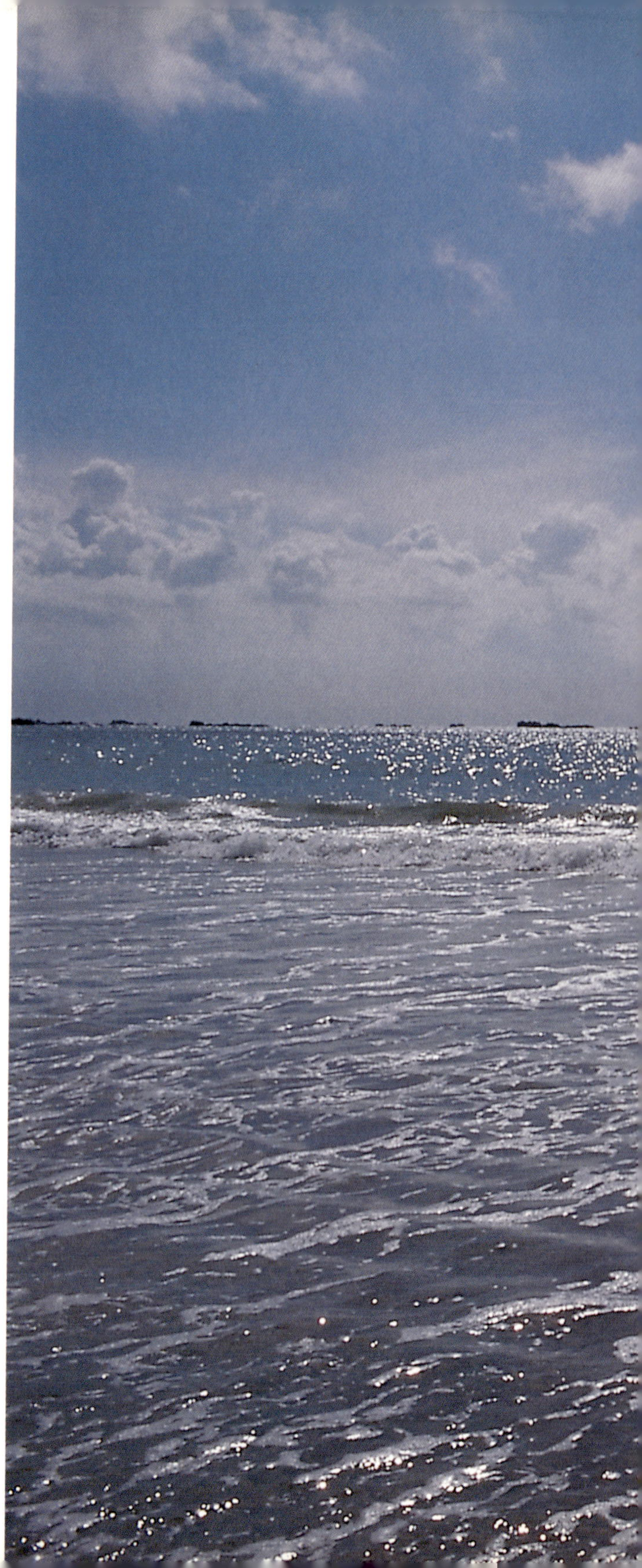

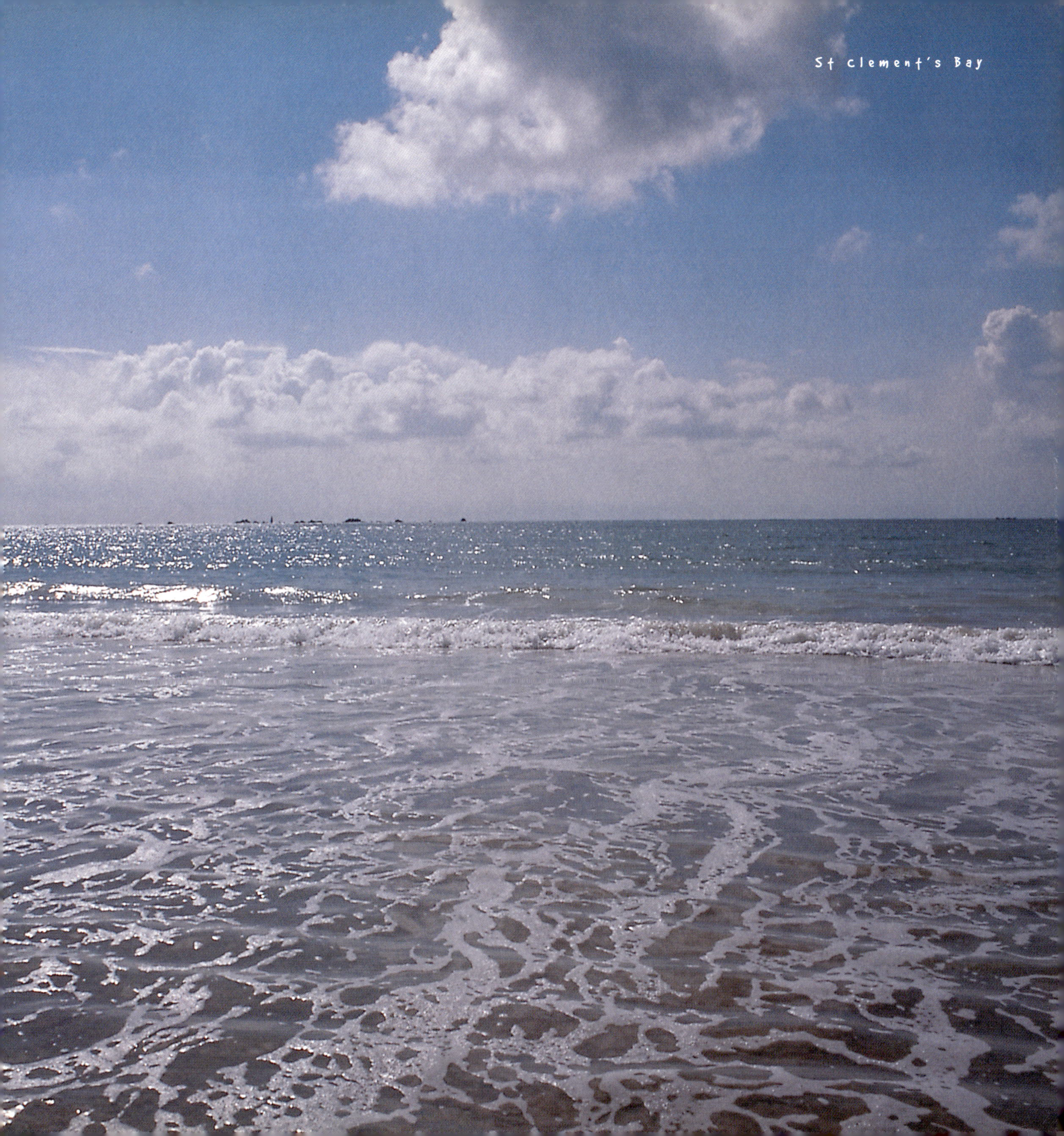
St Clement's Bay

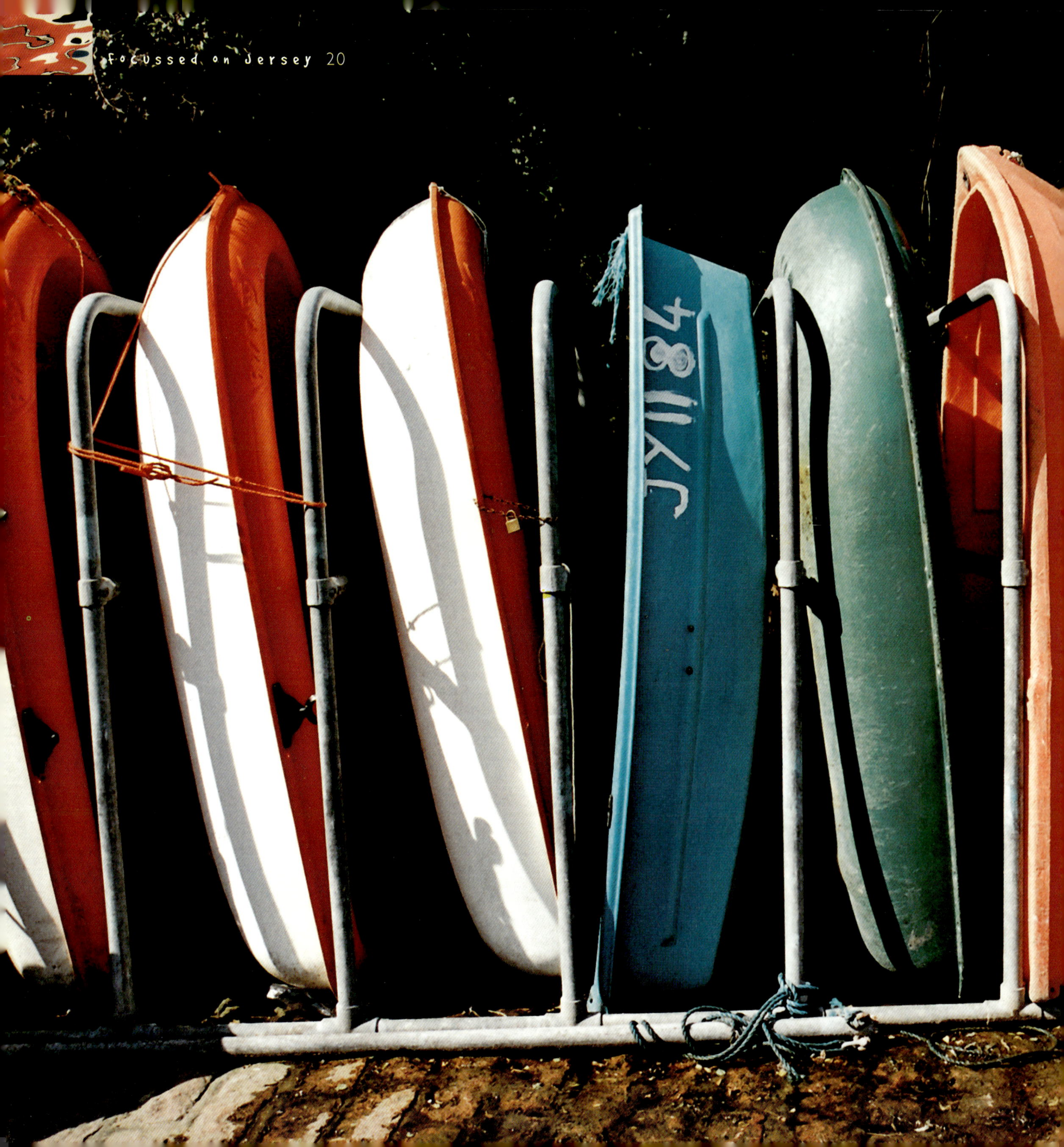

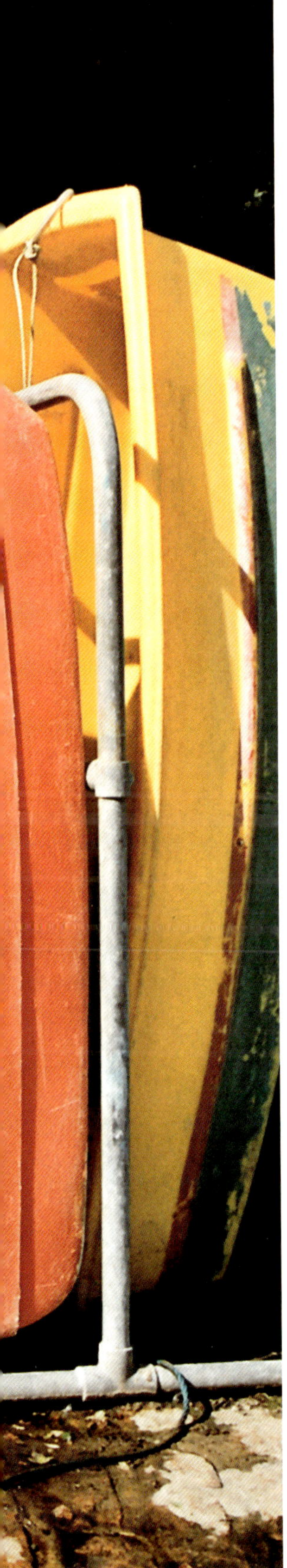

Royal Marines

By Jenny du Feu
Hautlieu

A line of soldiers
Tall and proud
Waiting patiently in the glistening sun
Waiting...
Waiting for orders.

They stand, eminent, on the exquisite granite of Jersey's coastline
They're ready...
Ready to face the island's cool, clear shimmering sea.

Behind them trees sway softly in the gentle breeze
The captain arrives...
Arrives to take them
They're eager to obey their orders and begin their journey.

Boats Stacked

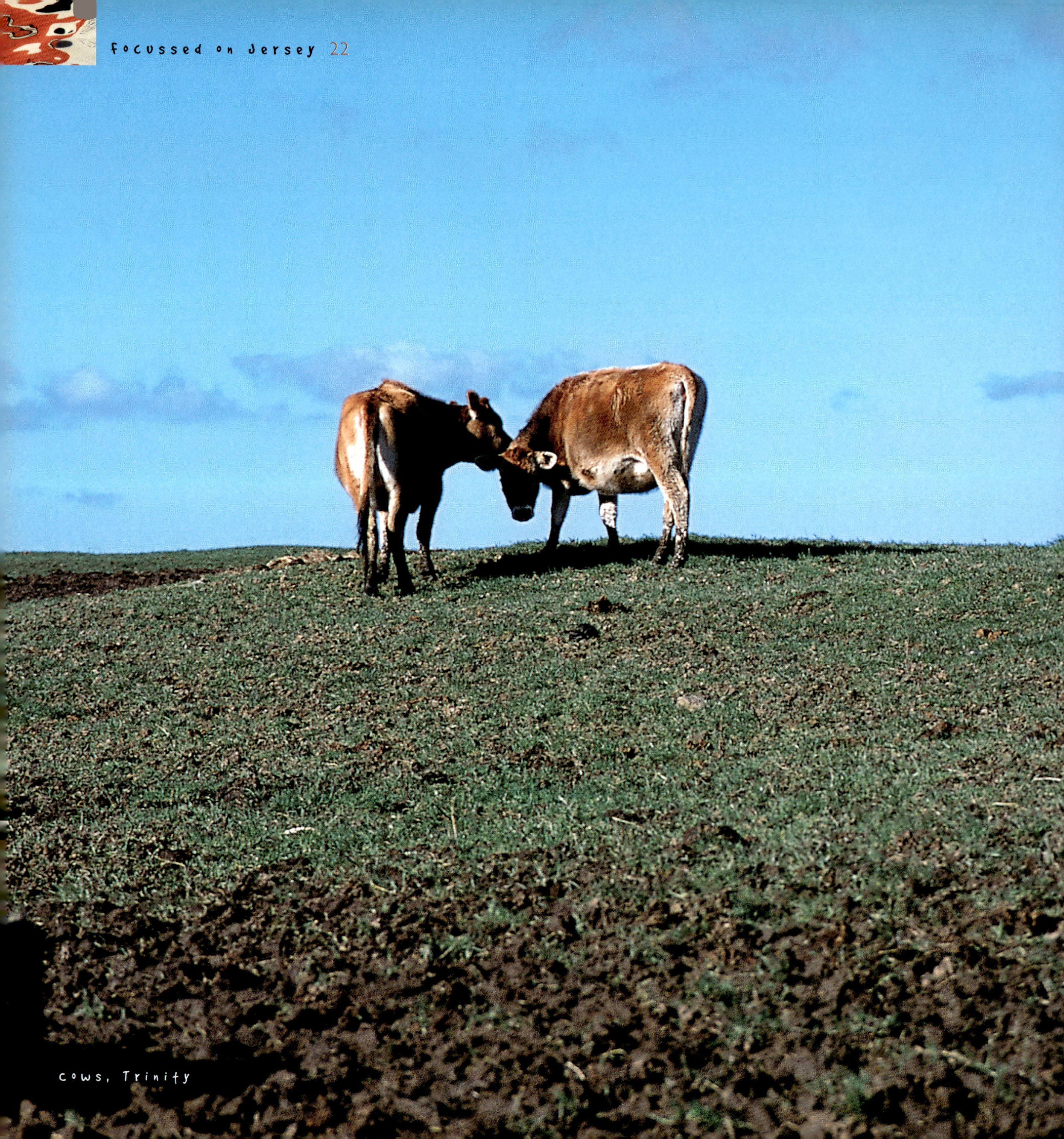

cows, Trinity

The Loyal Life

By Emma Brint

Beaulieu

From the mud, to the grass,
To the beast, to the sky;
Used for steak, for milk,
Or a Jersey beef pie.
Or not.
Could showing inspire the cows,
Or should one say the breeder?
Animals could have the privilege of freedom,
Yet they choose to be controlled by their owner, their leader.
Their strength so strong,
Their width so wide, the outer crust of mud and dust,
Their cleanliness to hide.
Dried grass slides down the animals' throat,
And so does the common weed,
Standing loyal upon the Jersey soil.
Awaiting their master dressed in tweed.

I am a Winkle

By Rebecca Michel
Quennevias

I am a winkle,
Upon a rock,
No one knows I exist,
People don't give a second thought about me,
I feel alone and rejected sometimes,
But when the glistening of the sun,
Sparkles on my soft, chalky shell,
It fills my home with warmth.
I am no better than any other winkle,
The only thing that makes me myself,
Is my detailed pattern on my shell,
Different colours, lines, dots,
They're mine,
As I sit on a rock.
No different from any other day,
My rubbery slippery body moves along,
The rigid, tough, rock,
No one really cares about me.
Winkle, what winkle? Who cares?
Then I'm gone,
My home, life and heart,
Stopped, crushed,
At the end of the day,
The sea covers me,
Like a blanket of clouds over the sky,
The cold salty water slips and slides into my shell,
As I go to sleep.

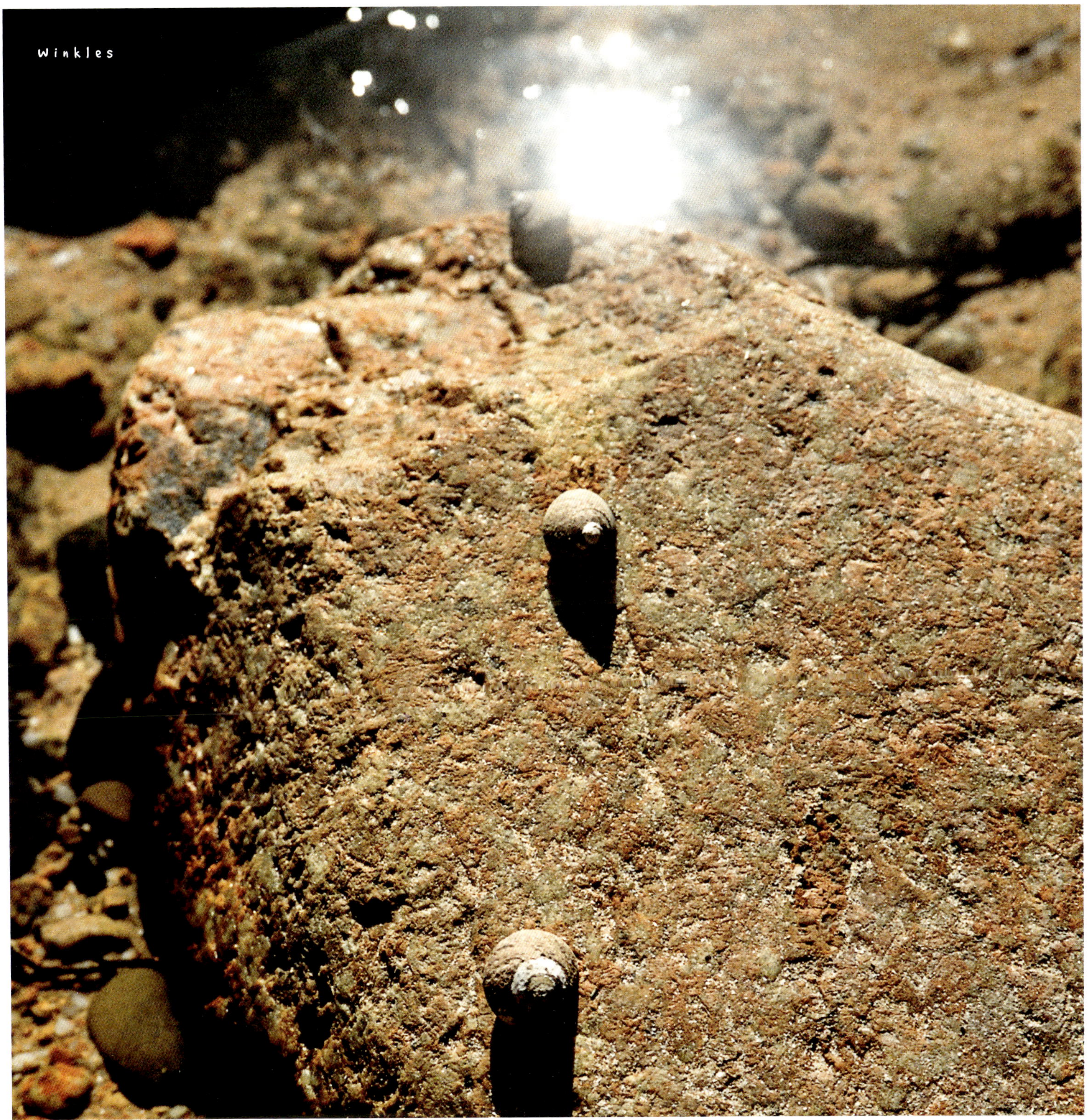
Winkles

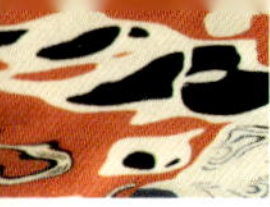

The Boat

By Duncan Poolton
Victoria College

Every day and every night,
I sail quietly over the glistening waves,
Not too fast not too slow,
Just sailing over the glistening waves:
Every day and every night,
I sail quietly with birds screeching,
Not too fast not too slow,
Just sailing with birds screeching.
Every day and every night,
I sail quietly with fish swimming,
Not too fast not too slow,
Just sailing with fish swimming.
Every day and every night,
I sail quietly into the harbour,
Not too fast not too slow,
Just sailing into the harbour.

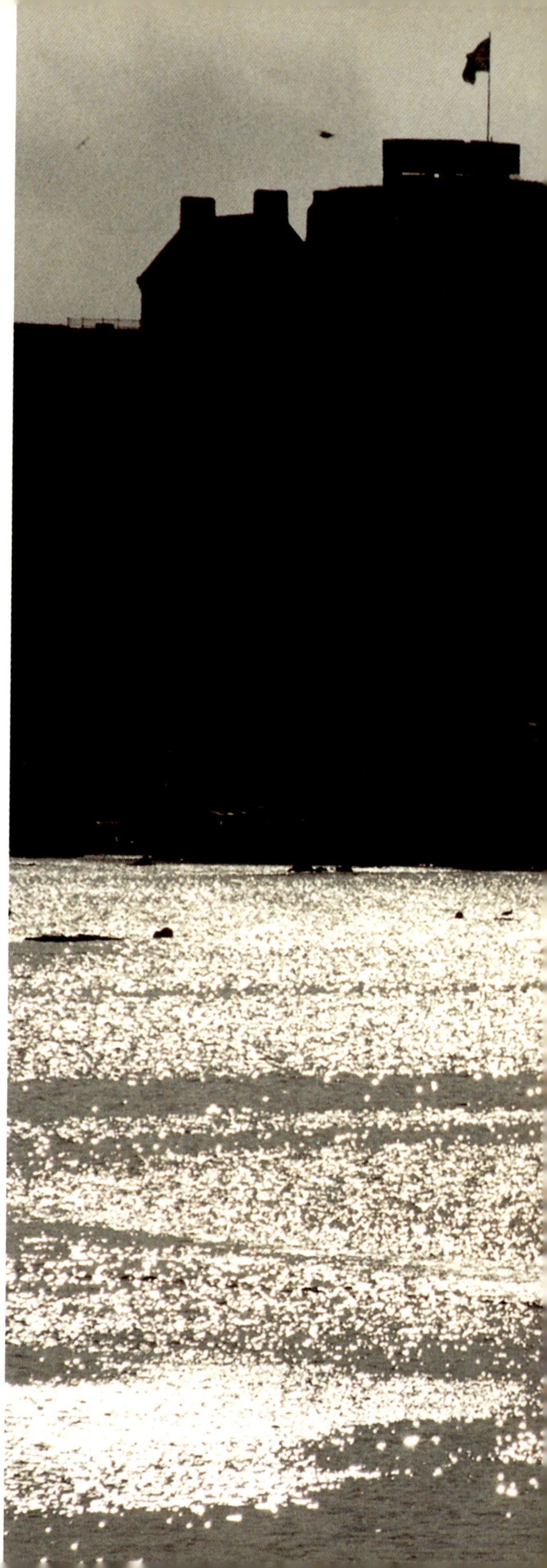

Elizabeth castle

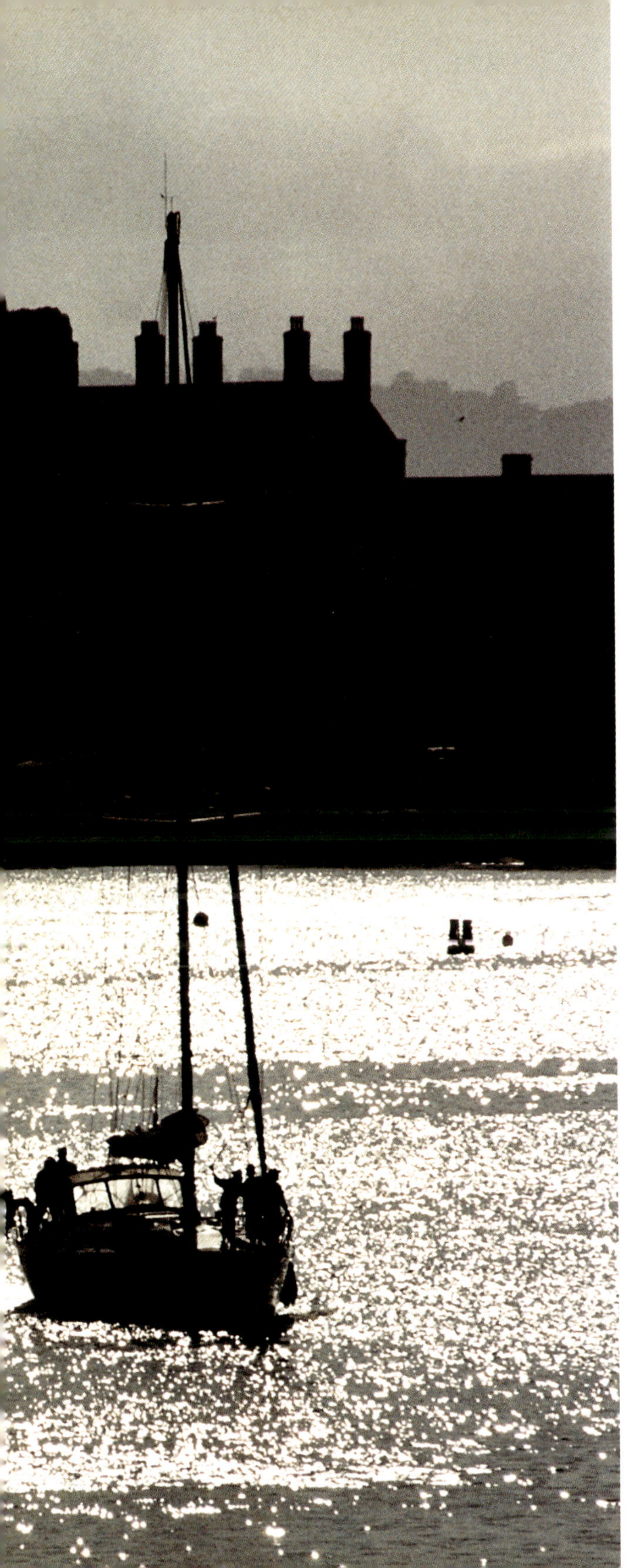

Untitled

By Ciara Mooney
Les Quennevais

Bathed in shades of gold and pink
Along the water I slink
Along the ripples that whisper so,
Sail away in your dreams
Along the gold waters find peace
The waters are calm, slick and smooth
Like the dreams I soothe
My hopes are strong, my dreams float high,
My fears and doubts swim on by
And suddenly a castle did rise
From the shining depths
Before my very eyes
A castle where dreams come true
Be anyone, do anything, is up to you
So for now, till my time is up
And I must return to roads and cars
People and work, concrete and tar,
I'll sail along in seas of gold and skies of blue
Being whoever I want to be
And do whatever I want to do.

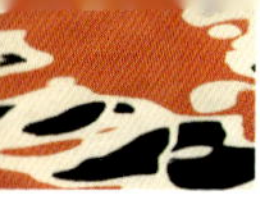

Beyond the shore

By Chloe Mattock
Jersey College for Girls

What is there beyond the shore?
Is there a land that is only for good?
With Palm trees and Oak trees and Birds of all colours.
Or snow topped mountains with Fir trees and Ice,
With Penguins and Bears of all kinds side by side.
A place with no prejudice,
A place to be free.
A place for happiness;
Is this place just beyond the shore, beyond the Sea?

What is there beyond the Shore?
Maybe an underwater paradise,
Where you swim all you like, and all the time you will see
All the creatures that reside under the sea.
With Turtles and Lobsters and all kinds of Crabs,
Or Fishes of colours you would never have known,
And Dolphins and Whales and even a Shark,
But all will be well,
For this is your underwater paradise.
Beyond the Shore. Beyond the Sea.
What is there Beyond the Shore?

Maybe a never-ending Ocean Blue,
Where you skate forever across the waves,
And touch all the stars in the Sky,
While singing the song of the sea with the moon or
whistling the Universes Lullaby.
Perhaps just once more we'll take a trip under the waves,
To play with the Seals,
And then you'll be back to skating the waves.
BEYOND THE SHORE!

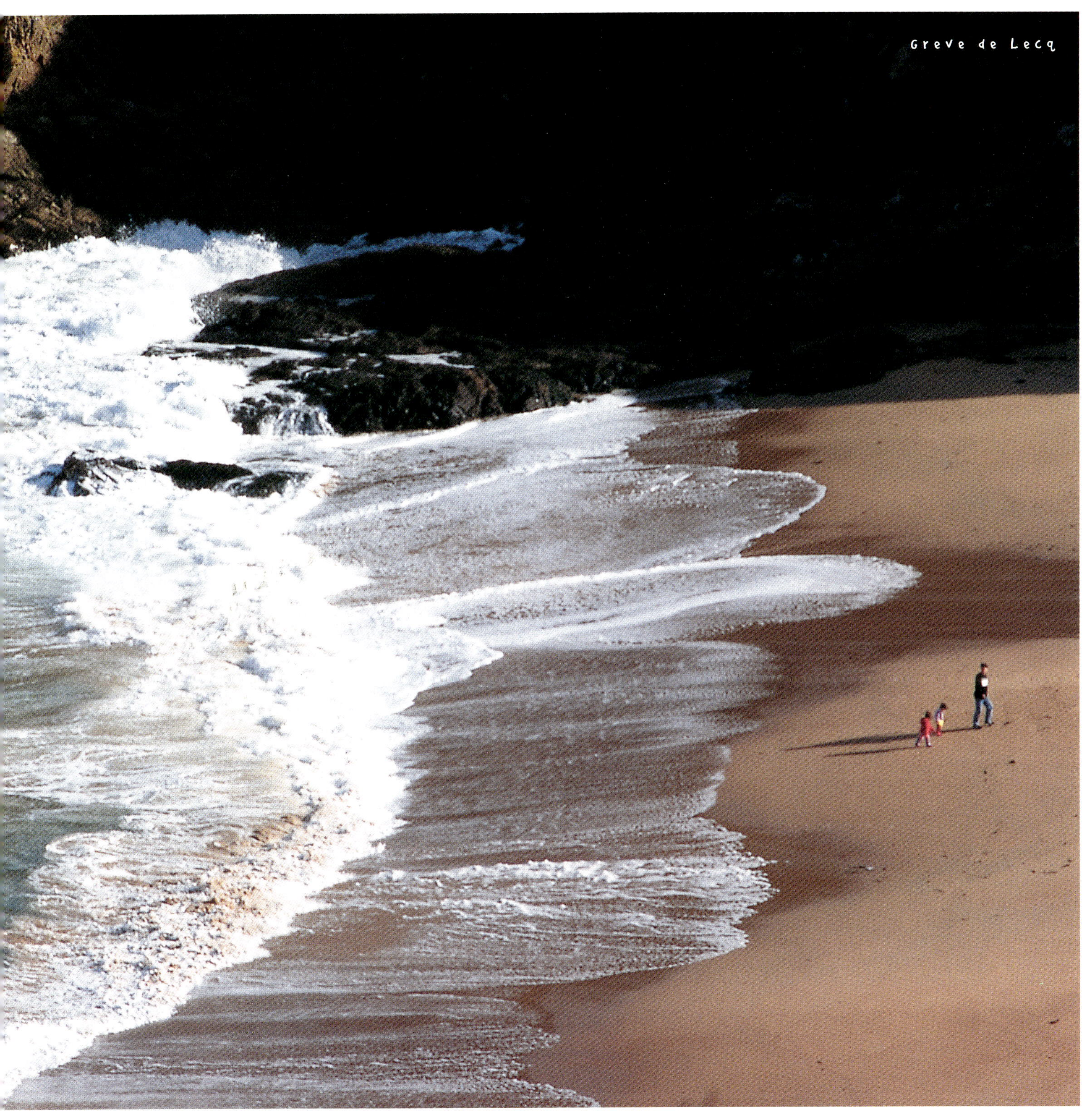
Greve de Lecq

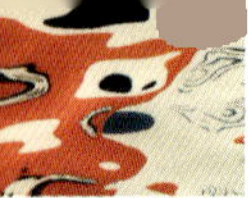

Untitled

By Leanne Le Feuvre
Les Quennevais

The lighthouse
Has been there for years
Just think of all them memories
Of the war that brought tears.

The white building as tall as a steeple
Was built there to protect Jersey's people,
By the doorway it looks a bit red
But really it could be a dead person's bed.

In summer the children play on the sand
In front of the lighthouse that
once was a warland.
They don't realise the things this
lighthouse has seen,
The date on the wall brings back
memories harsh and mean.

Jersey Poem - old and New

By Richard Brooks
Hautlieu

The light fades to dark,
Looming stone hard and cold,
Moist with the sea's churning,
Rough and uneven still held firm,
As the loan sea gull looks on.
Reaching into the eternal sky,

The strong, menacing metal stanchions,
The reassuringly sturdy ladder,
Stretching up to the light,
Where the sea gull looks on.

The curving wall of stone,
Engraved with age,
Still strong, still standing,
Seemingly never to die,
While the sea gull looks on.

Could the stanchions last as long?
Could they outlive the rock on
which they stand,
Which sustains the ocean pounding?
Ageing stone or polished steel?
You decide, while the sea gull looks on!

St catherine's Lighthouse

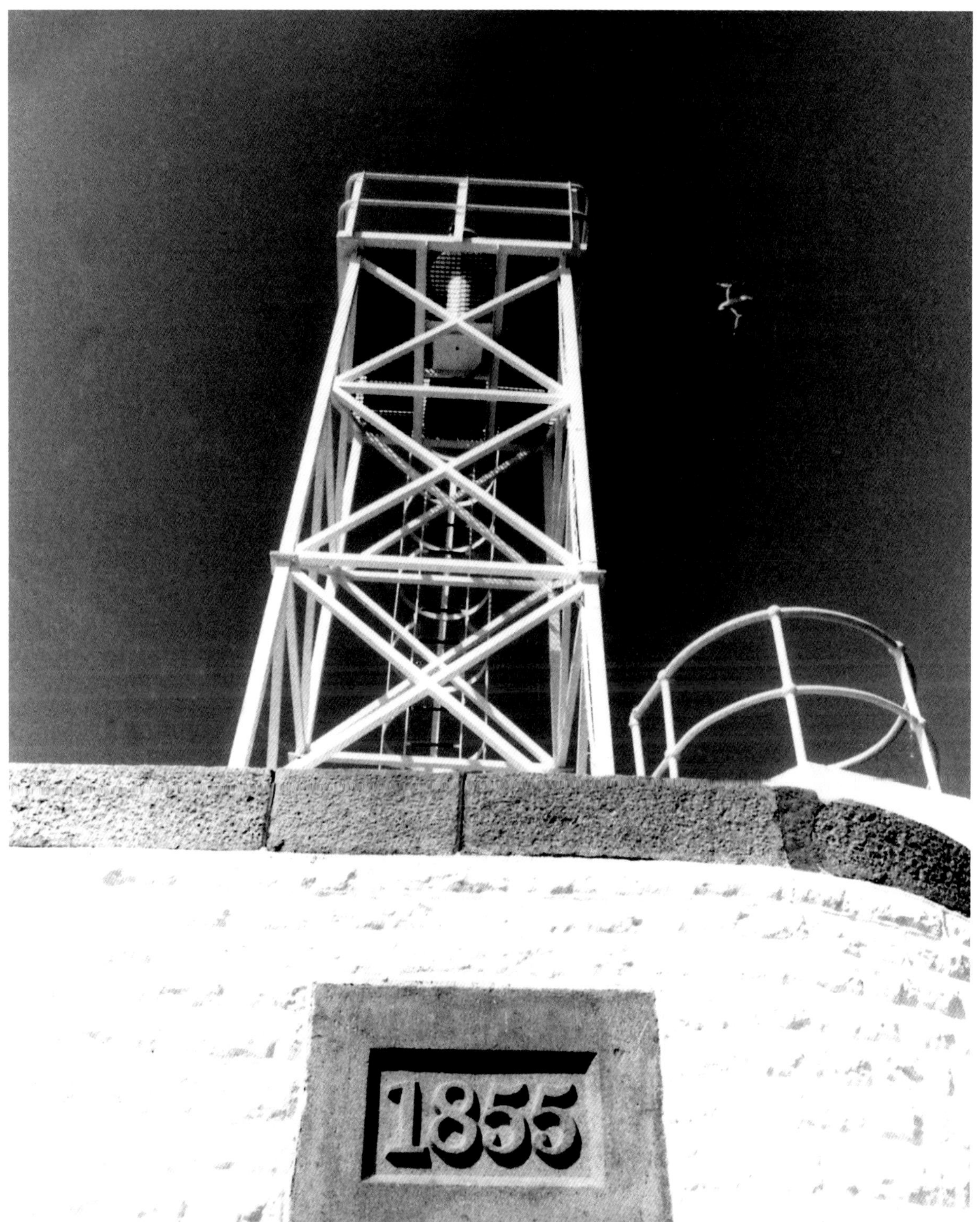
1855

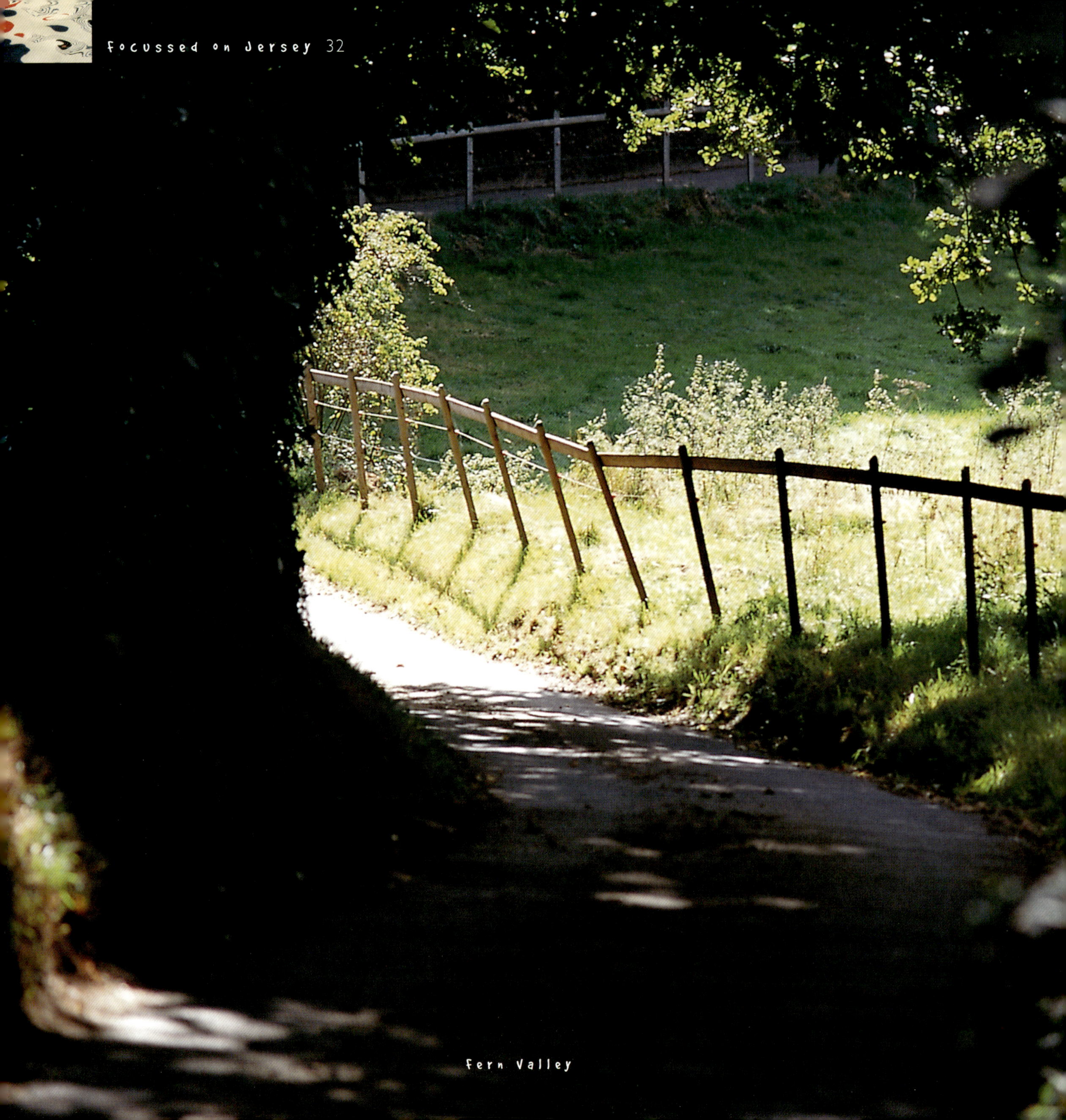

Fern Valley

Going forward to the past

By Mairi Hare

Beaulieu

I walk down the country lane,
Slowly, step by step.
Memories crawling back to me,
From the history of my life.
The rickety old fence – still hasn't collapsed,
And the ivy-covered tree;
Where we used to have our picnics,
A feast of cake and tea.
Light trickles through the leaves,
of the old, great oak;
Like it has done from years before,
From the past to the present, for evermore.
We played games of many kinds,
And tried to walk the fence.
I guess we damaged it quite a bit,
That's why it is out of place.
This lane holds many memories
Both happy, and sad,
It hasn't changed, it's still the same,
But there's just one thing missing.
It's quiet at the moment,
Just wait and see.
Because now the winter has died away,
And the children have come back to play.

The Path to Nowhere

By Melissa Male

Les Quennevais

A secret pathway to a
tranquil place,
The other side shines like
silky lace,
How will I get to this
other side?
Through shadowed darkness
where old ghosts hide,
A noisy rustle in the golden
leaves here and there,
This path is deserted, does
anybody care?
That there could be a whole
new world for us,
Where the sun shines all day
without a fuss,
Does it lead directly into the
shimmering sea?
There is a comforting place,
waiting for you and for me.

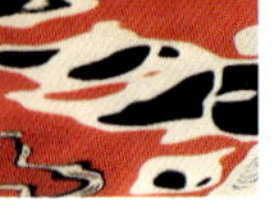

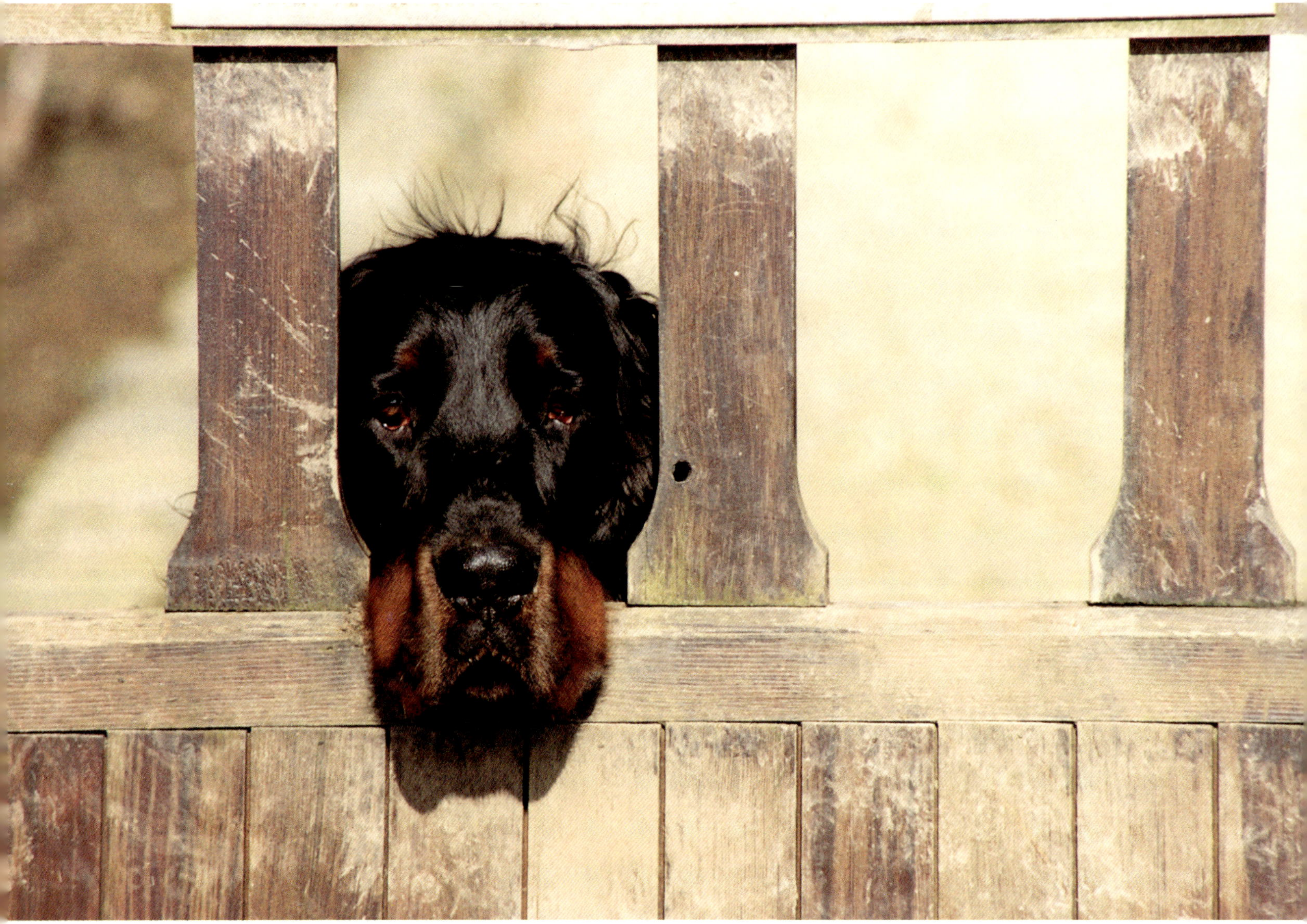

Watchdog, Trinity

A Dog's Dream

By Charlotte Ireson

St George's

Why should I be locked up all day
Nowhere to run nowhere to play?
All I see is cars rushing by
Day by day. I just look out of my
Wooden gate looking at everyone
Who's got freedom.

Should a dog sit behind a gate
Doing nothing?
I ask these questions for one reason
I want to get out through this gate to freedom?

Untitled

Laura Battrick

Les Quennevais

I sit, my head pressed between the bars,
I listen, for people or passing cars,
I watch, the early sunrise each day
I have my place, I sit I stay.
Busy men with their wives,
Have to take care of their mundane lives
I am always watching, but am never watched, I am
not noticed I am not touched.
They're all too busy to come and play
So I have my place I sit, I stay.

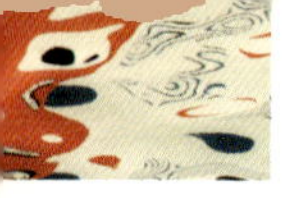

It's Like Heaven!

By Gaby Skelley
Grainville

So Calm!
A silhouette waits in the water's shades
While day rests, and dusk emerges.
The serrated rocks surround and protect the
Black picture painted across the water.
It's like heaven, so quiet, so calm, so clear.

The silhouette, it's lonely, it's cold,
Waits for the owner to return,
They'll be back, they always are,
Ready for the day's work again.
It's like heaven, so quiet, so calm, so clear.

So Clear!
The black rock islands sit scattered around me,
They never talk, and they never move,
But I know they're not angry for me
trespassing their space,
It's like heaven, so quiet, so calm, so clear.

I must rest now, in my peaceful waters,
It's so perfect here, this is my home.
My friends, the silent, motionless rocks,
And my owner, the one that awakes my peace
It's like heaven, so quiet, so calm, so clear.

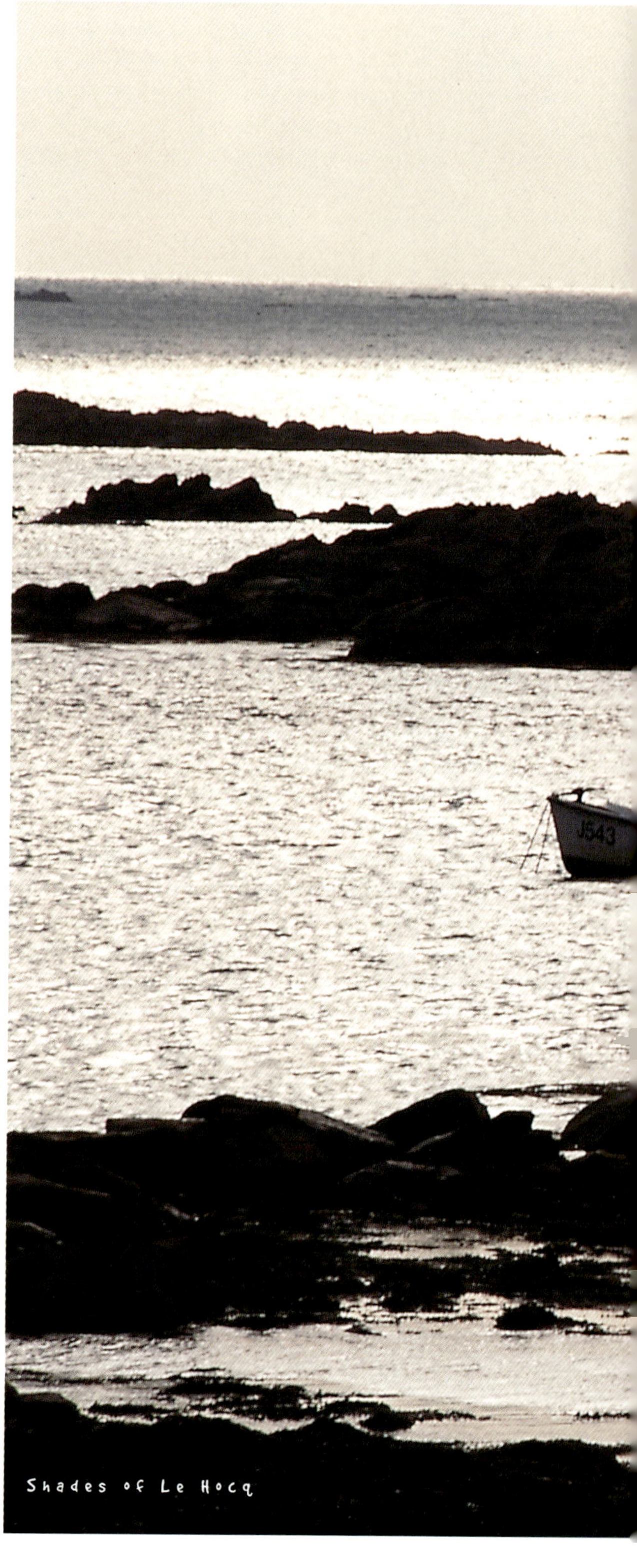

Shades of Le Hocq

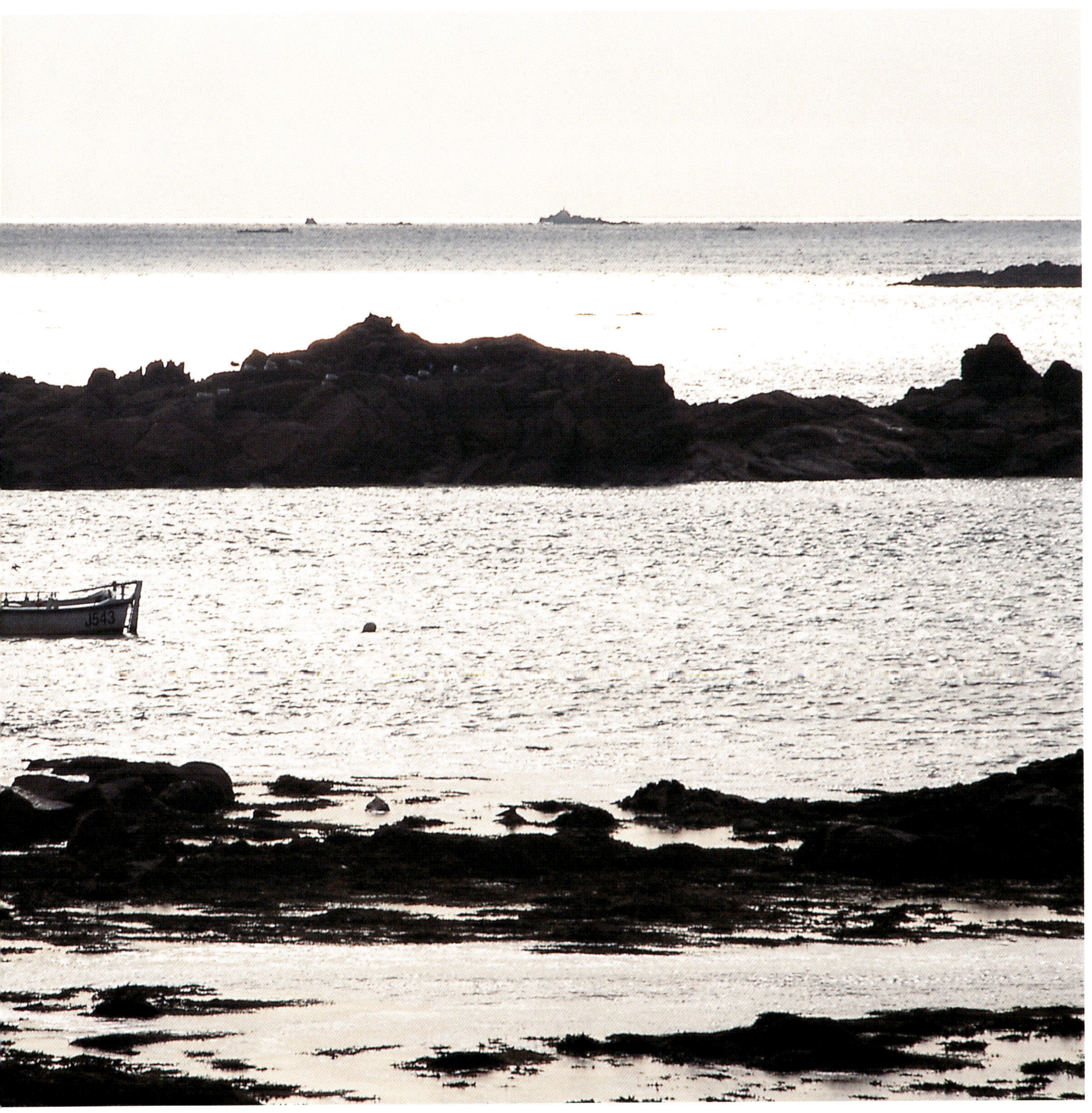
J543

Priorities

By Mathew Robin
Hautlieu

Dollars, Euros. Pounds and Yen,
What are they worth?
Are the markets soaring or crashing?
Are we buying or selling?
Borrowing or lending?
Are we over budget, out of time?
Are we late for the meeting, in line for a raise?
On course for a promotion?
Dollars, Euros, Pounds and Yen,
What are they worth?
Our jobs, our lives?
STOP!

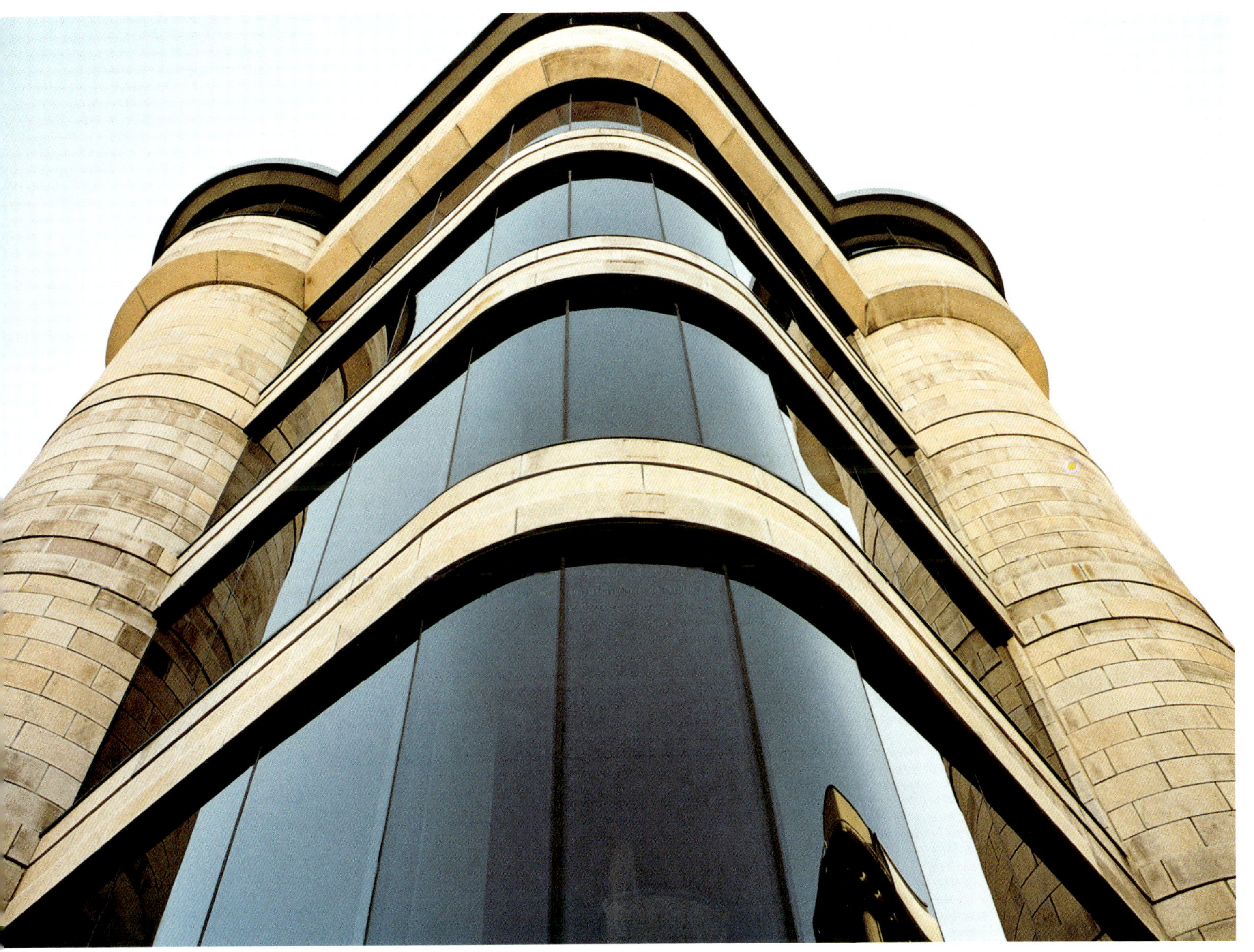

Tower Block

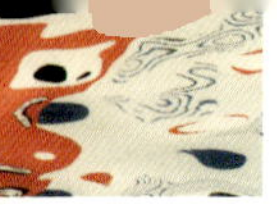

This iron chain

By Laura Finney
and Rebecca Williamson
Les Quennevais

You look at this chain
And think
Nothing.
This iron chain
Links,
The past,
The present
And the future.

Someone, somewhere,
Created it
With few tools,
And hard effort.
This chain has
Secured boats from
Sinking in stormy
Seas

How old is this chain?
Does any body care?
It must be old as it
Bleeds orange
Over the stony
Bay.
It'll out live
This generation
And others to come.

Can you imagine how many
people it has seen during
Its time, enjoying
Themselves
Upon this
Very
Bay.
How
Many
People have
Walked on past
Without giving it a look?

Fisherman's Tie

By Sophie Gaber
Beaulieu

Fisherman's wedding ring
to the Island,
His grip to the land,
The lock to his home,
The ring remains loyal to her master's hand,
Never leaving her master, never leaving the sea.

She's the first to pull him in at night,
The last to bid farewell when light.
She's the place his ship turns to when in need.
Her strong influences to his heart
Can even capture his roaring speed.
Her simple beauty never fails
To draw the boats in,
The ever-returning sails
Flood the harbour in.

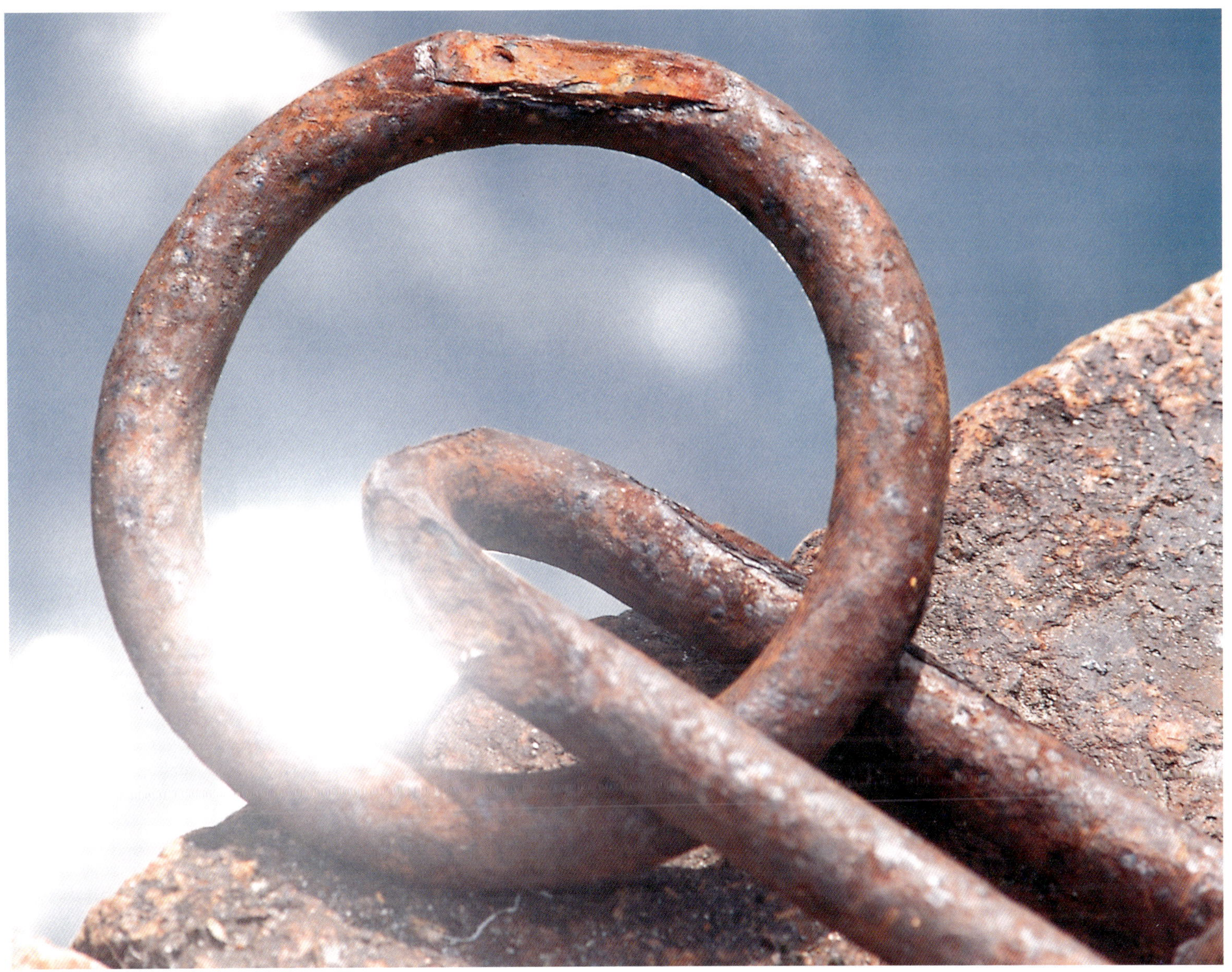

Mooring Ring

She bears witness to the secrets of the storm,
She delights at the sights of a calm summer's day,
Following her master only by thought when at bay.

She keeps her master dry and grounded
Whilst he drifts into a world of his own.
His mind at rest, never alone.

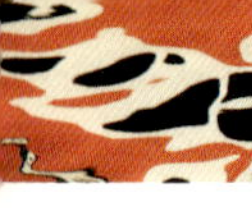

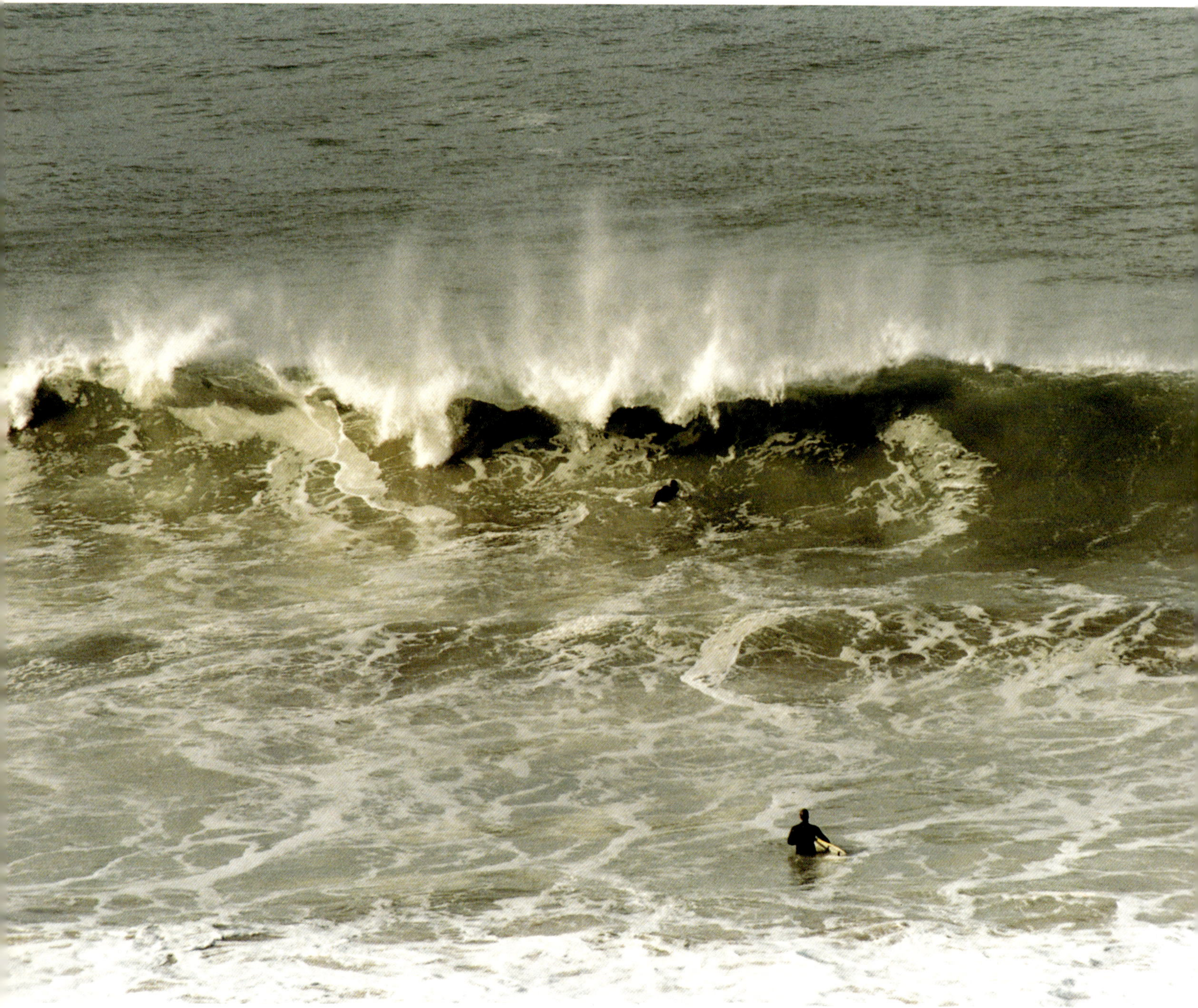

Plemont Surfers

The Sea

By Bryony Le Boutillier
Jersey College for Girls

The sea, the sea it rolls and waves
And deep below in cracks and caves
Fish will glide and seaweed sway
And out to sea the dolphins play.

The sea is like an angry bear
The storm will rip and rage and tear
White horses race across the sands
Their roar is heard across the land.

The sea is like a purring cat
Stroking the sand and pebbles flat
As children play around the beach
The world of sea is out of reach.

The sea, the sea it waves and rolls
And deep below in nooks and holes
Is where the silent fishes play
I will return another day.

Untitled

By Shelley Vibert
Les Chenes

You can feel the waves crashing over
your head
Hoping you come out alive
You dread the day you'll die
But you know it will happen one day
Hoping it's not in the sea
Hoping not here not now
You can start to feel the coldness
The waves are getting stronger
You catch a wave back to shore
You know it's safer there
You go back again and again
The adrenaline rush is always there.

Reflections of a Boat

By Chantelle Arnold
Beaulieu

It's a clear summer's day,
In the Royal Bay.
Boats on water sailing by,
Blue sea reflected from the sky.
But I'm here, quite still,
Until my owner comes back from Grouville.
I'm in the shadow of Mont Orgueil,
Watching the French coast close by.
He's having lunch at the Grill,
And then walking down Gorey Hill.
I'm part of the beautiful scene,
For the many tourists who have been.
I'm tied up tight so I don't fly away,
I expect to leave some time today.
Probably some time soon,
Before I'm shadowed by the moon.

Untitled

By Oliver Harrison and Craig Beeley
Haute Valleé

Many people do not think
The water that you drink
Can cause colours in a reflection.

One reflection could sing a song
And tell a story so long
Or make a picture out of nothing.

On the water the boats await
For the men with their bait
To go far, far away.

As the tide goes in and out
The boats sway all about
And the reflection comes and goes.

When it's in, the fish follow
Looking for food then they go
And they live under the reflection.

But when it's out and the boats lay low
The mud and stone underneath show
And the reflection is no more.

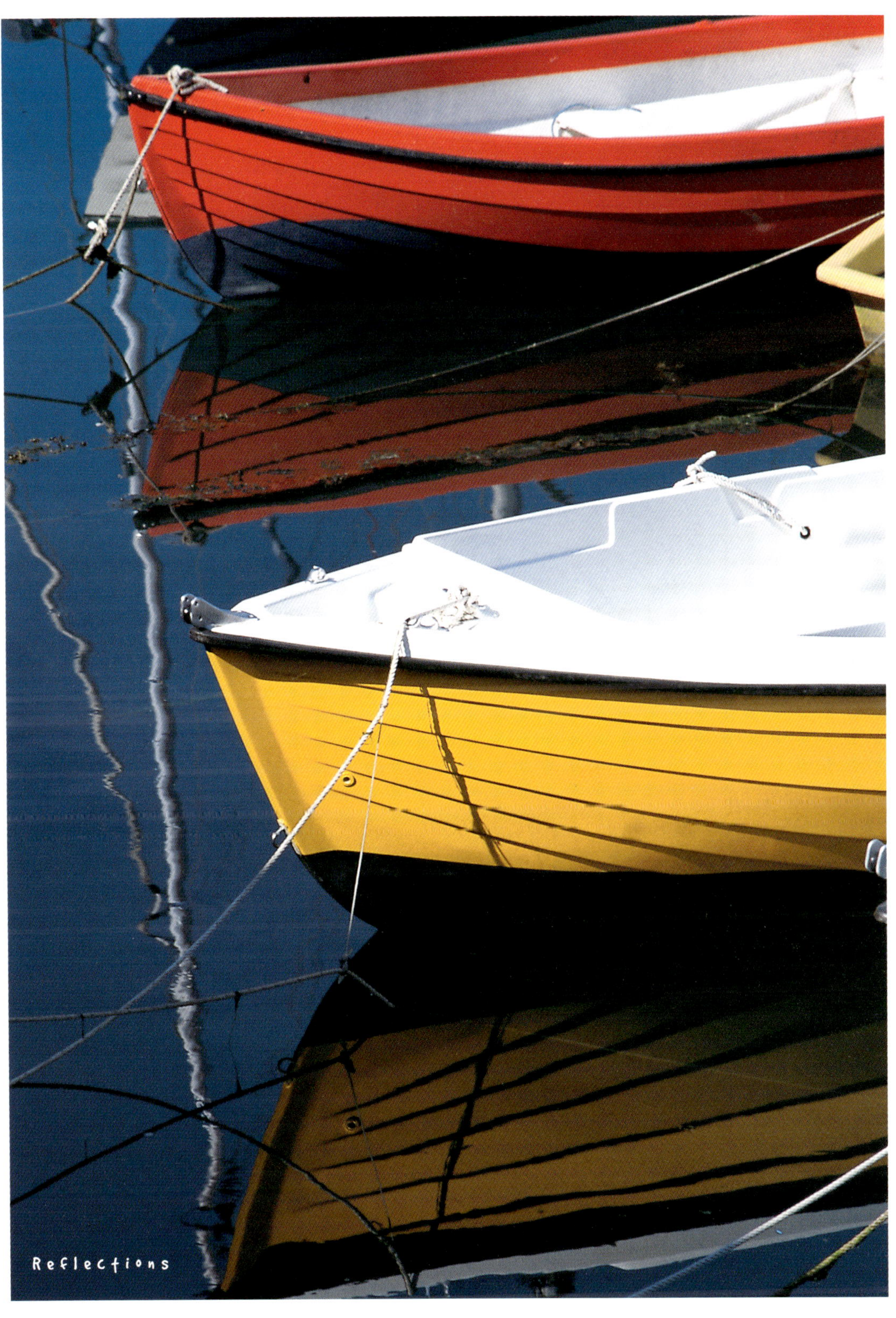

Reflections

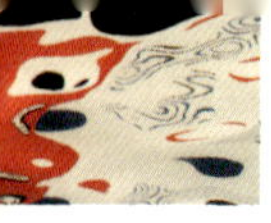

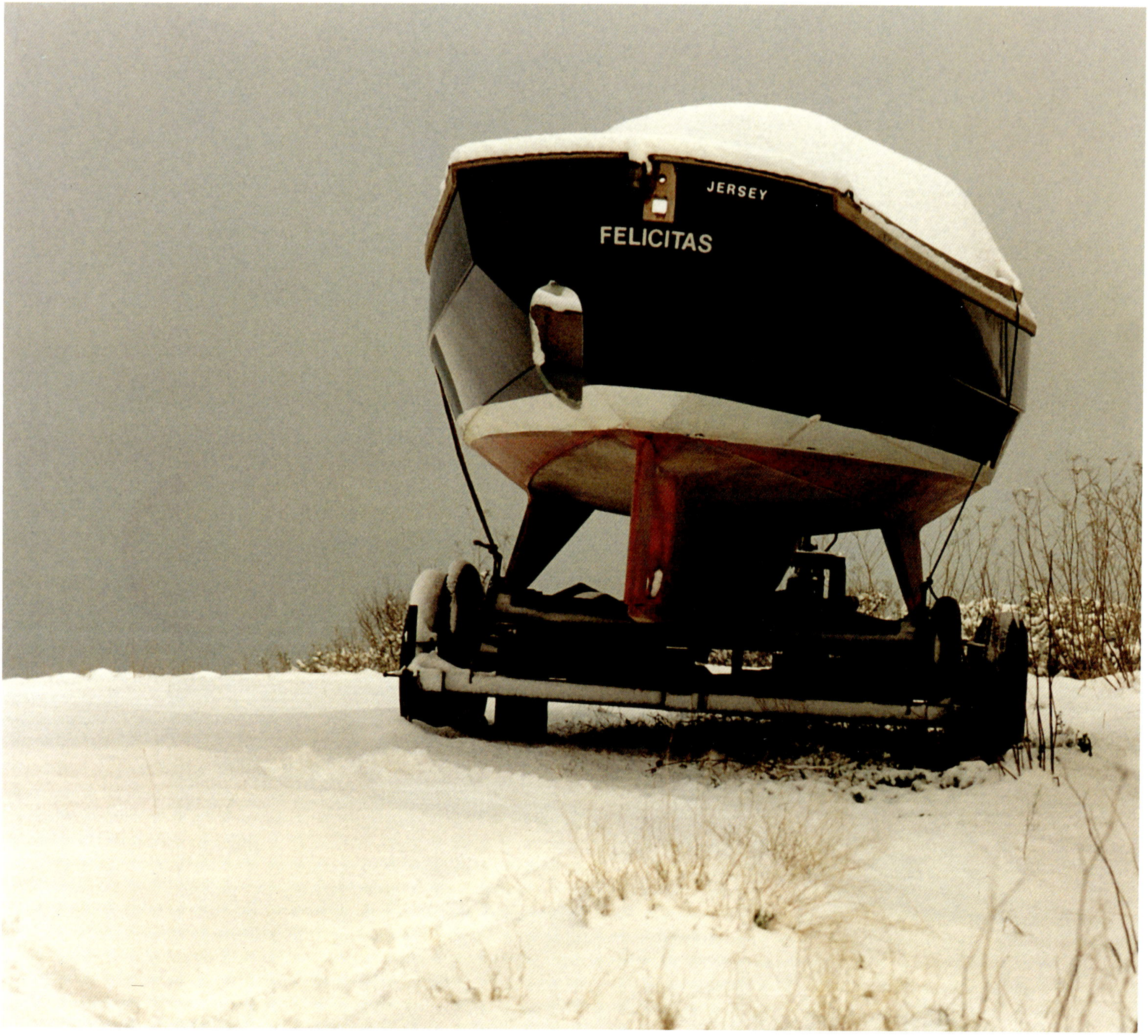

Felicitas

I am the Blue Boat

By Bryony Koester
Le Rocquier

I am the Blue Boat.

Here I am with all my mates,
Waiting for my fisherman with bait,
I am the Blue Boat.

Why won't my fisherman come
And take me to the sea again?
I am the bored Blue Boat.

Felicitas is my given name;
Sunday fishing was my game,
I am the sad Blue Boat.

The red and white racing boats,
Sit and jeer at me,
I am the slow Blue Boat.

I'll sit here through the winter,
Collecting all the rust and splinters,
I am the Blue Boat.

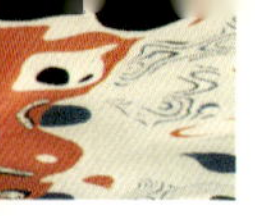

The Sunset

By Joe Mooney
Grainville

The clouds high up are rolling by,
An orange sunset is in the sky
The birds take flight along the bay
At the end of a beautiful day
The sun is setting in the sky.

This mighty sunset wears a crown
It won't be back until its dawn,
A rock may have been thrown too give them
A boost,
And off they go for a long night's roost,
The sun is going down.

So what happens when it is night,
When we're in bed all snug and tight?
What happens when the suns gone down,
Like us trying not to drown?

What happens when the sun is gone here comes the night.
Well I'm not going to tell like a crab in his shell,
But look at this picture you see
The photo of the rippling sea
The sun is the highest in our realm.

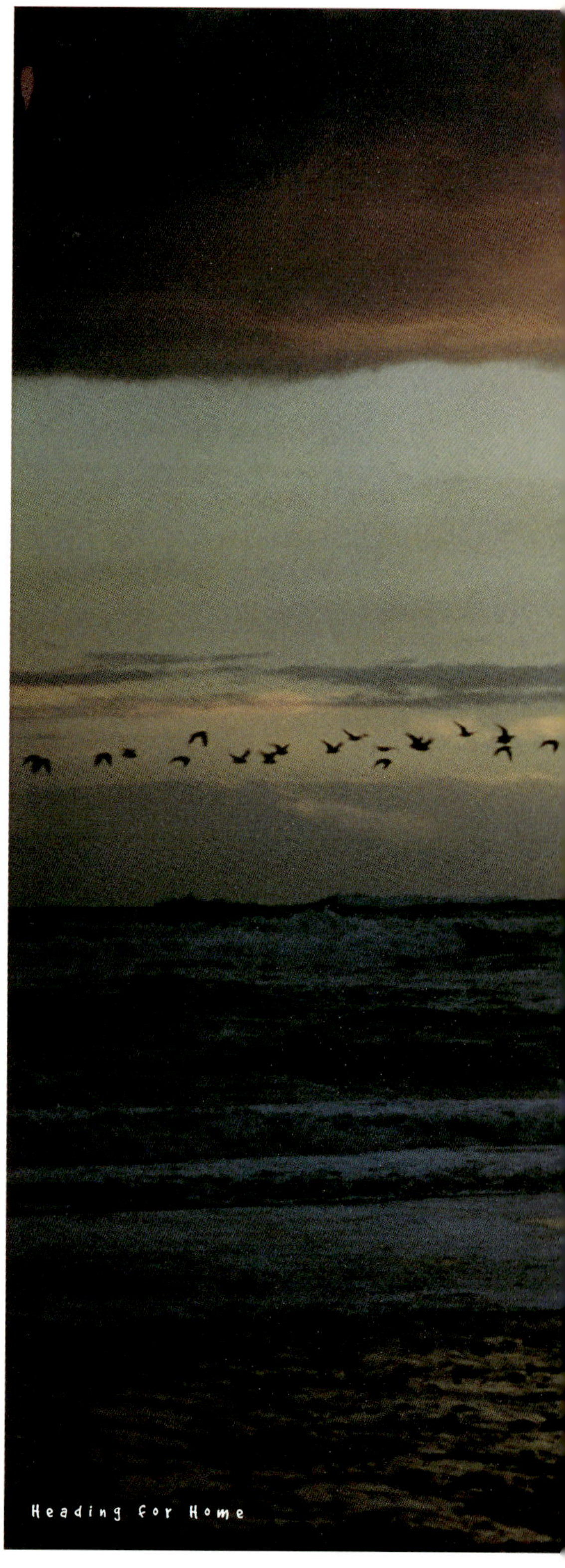
Heading for Home

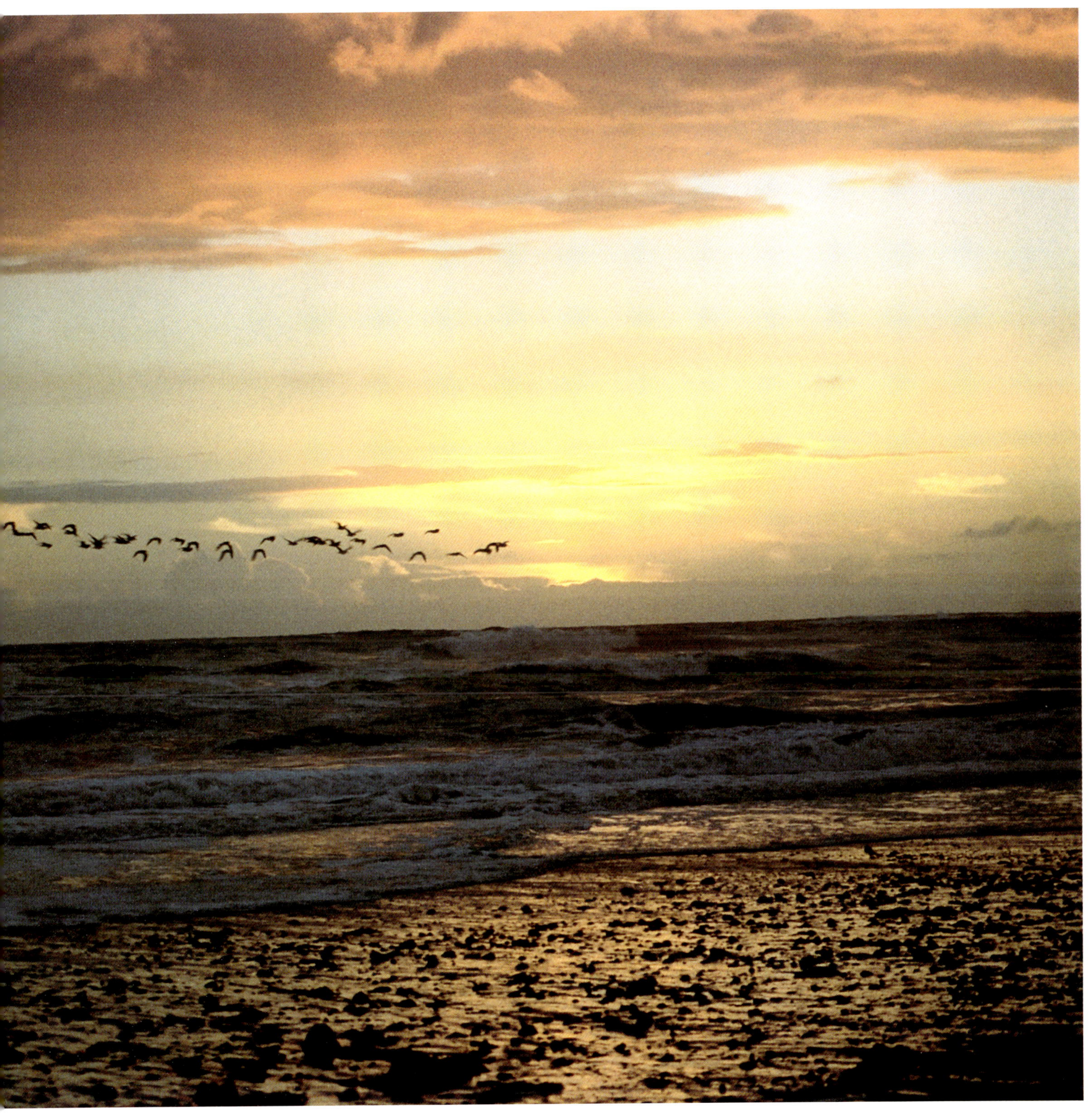

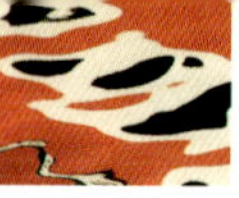

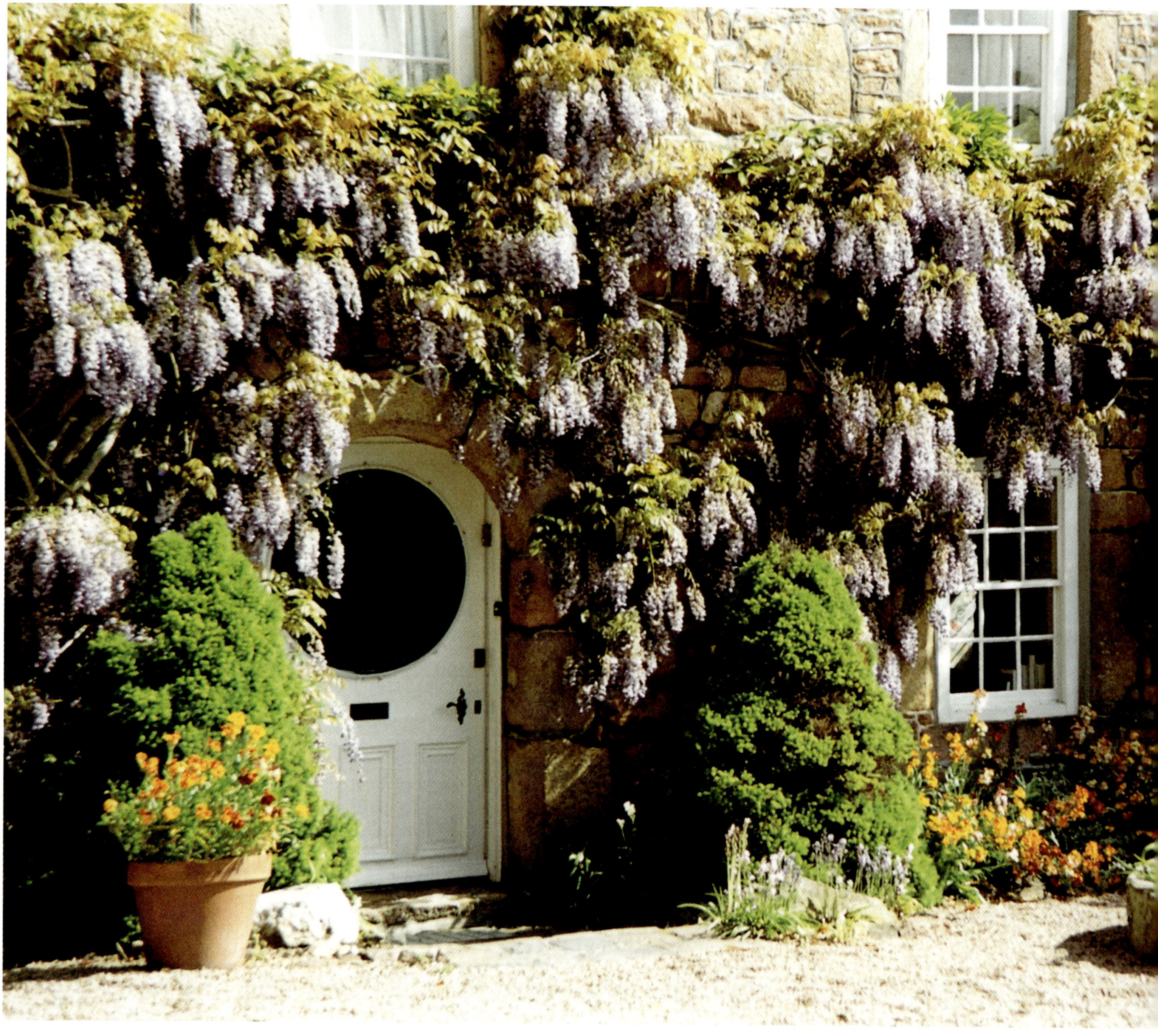

wisteria

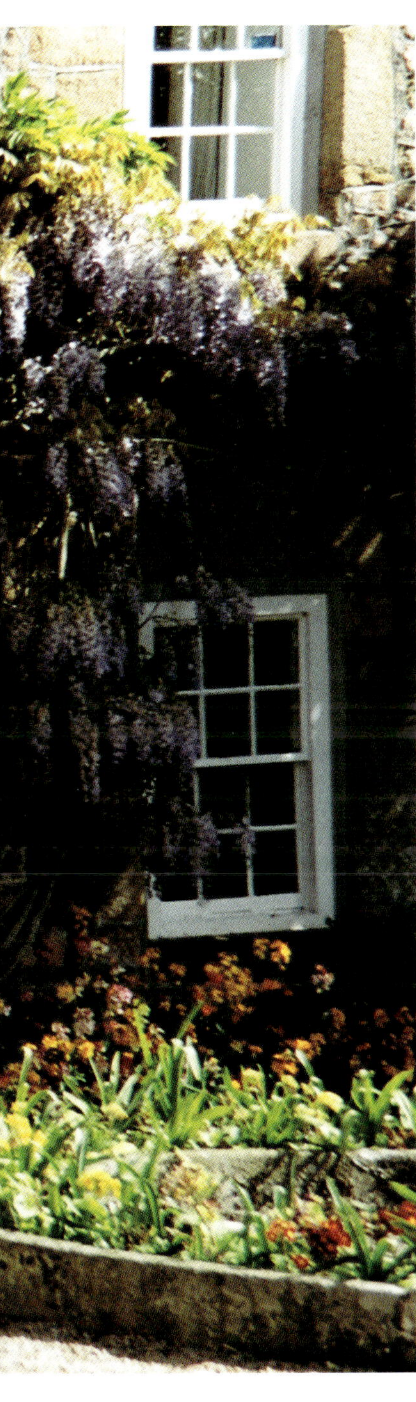

Sharing Whispers

By Katie Mason

Jersey College for Girls

Again the paper boy arrives
He's the only thread of life that visits
Delivering news from the outside world
Bringing our world alive

The gravel crunches under my feet
A floral scent pervades the air
The worn letter box lifts lightly
I wonder curiously what's inside

Left in silence once again
Warm rays of sun shine in
Memories of happy summer days,
Soft sand and foaming seas

I haven't got time to stand and stare
But still I wonder what lies in there
Hidden by the abundance of flowers
Old stone walls and secret door

Plemont-Another Place

(To be read in a Jersey accent)

By Alex Watson

De La Salle

When the tides half up
Bi Cri it's great,
Like an island of its own
But soon the tide will
Touch the wall and make
The rocks so prone
To waves that crash
And cause a splash
Far up the Café wall.
When the tide goes down
All is peace again
Except for a dog and his
bouncy ball.

Plemont

By Stephan Metcalfe

De La Salle

Plemont, a different world.
The strong rocks stand-alone,
Like Martello towers,
Protecting the world of the vast ocean.

A deep underworld beckons
Beneath the stony, granite shallows.
At high tide the beach is swamped
In the marvellous waves it is swallowed.

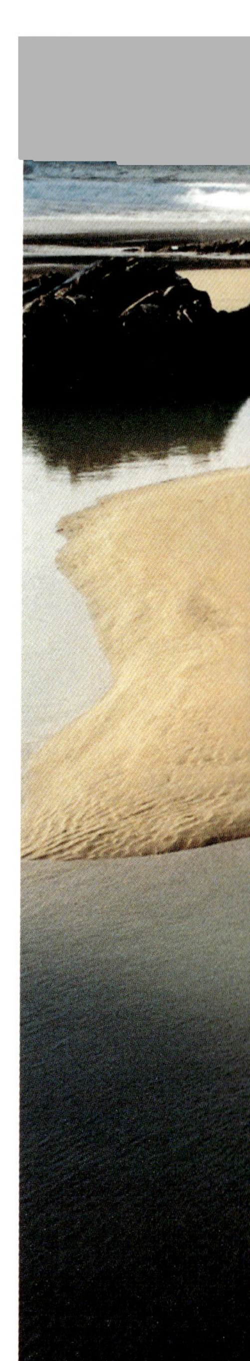

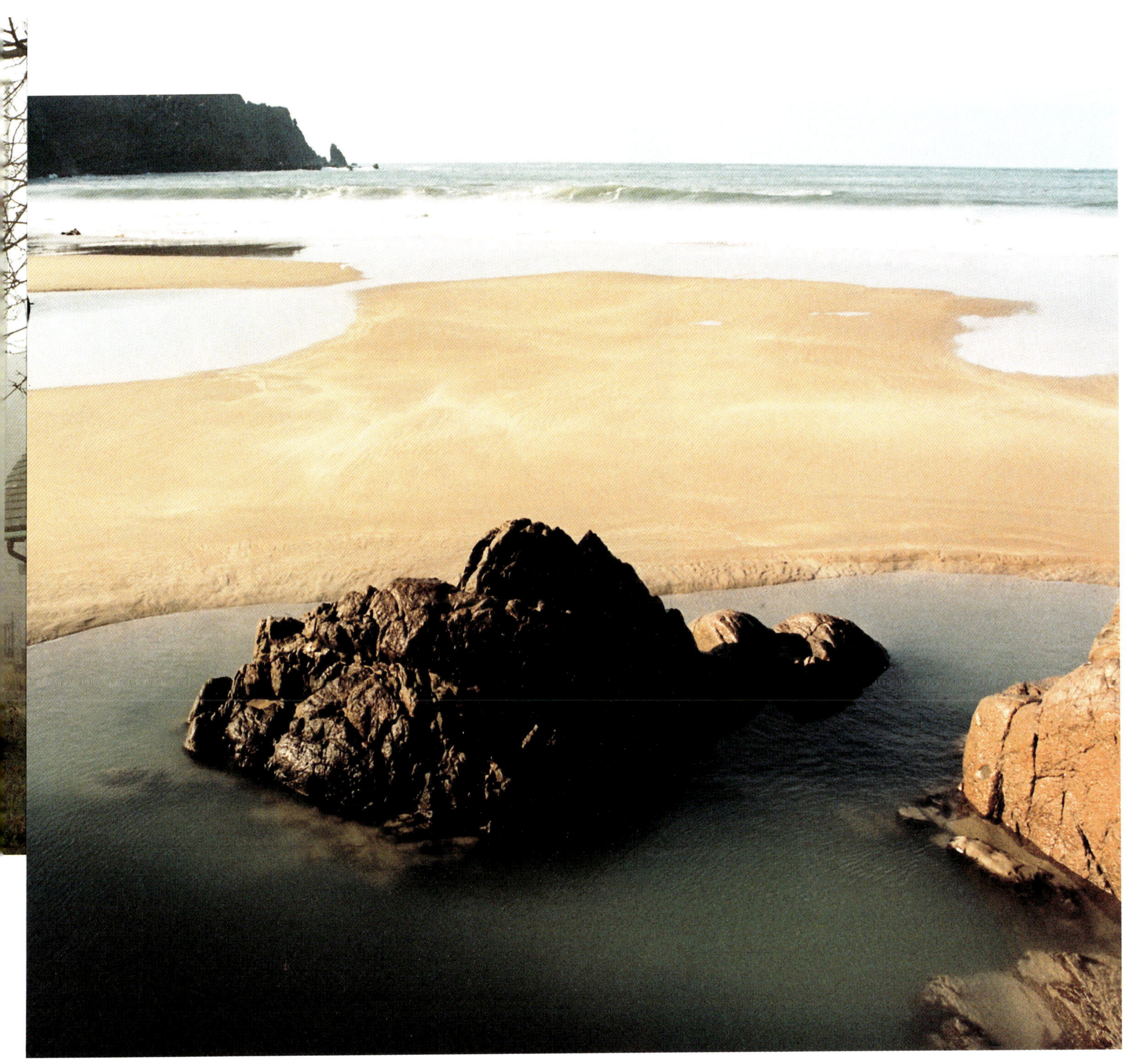

Plemont Beach

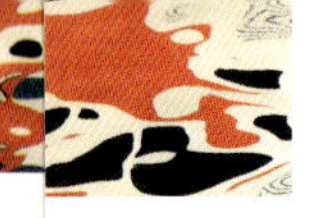

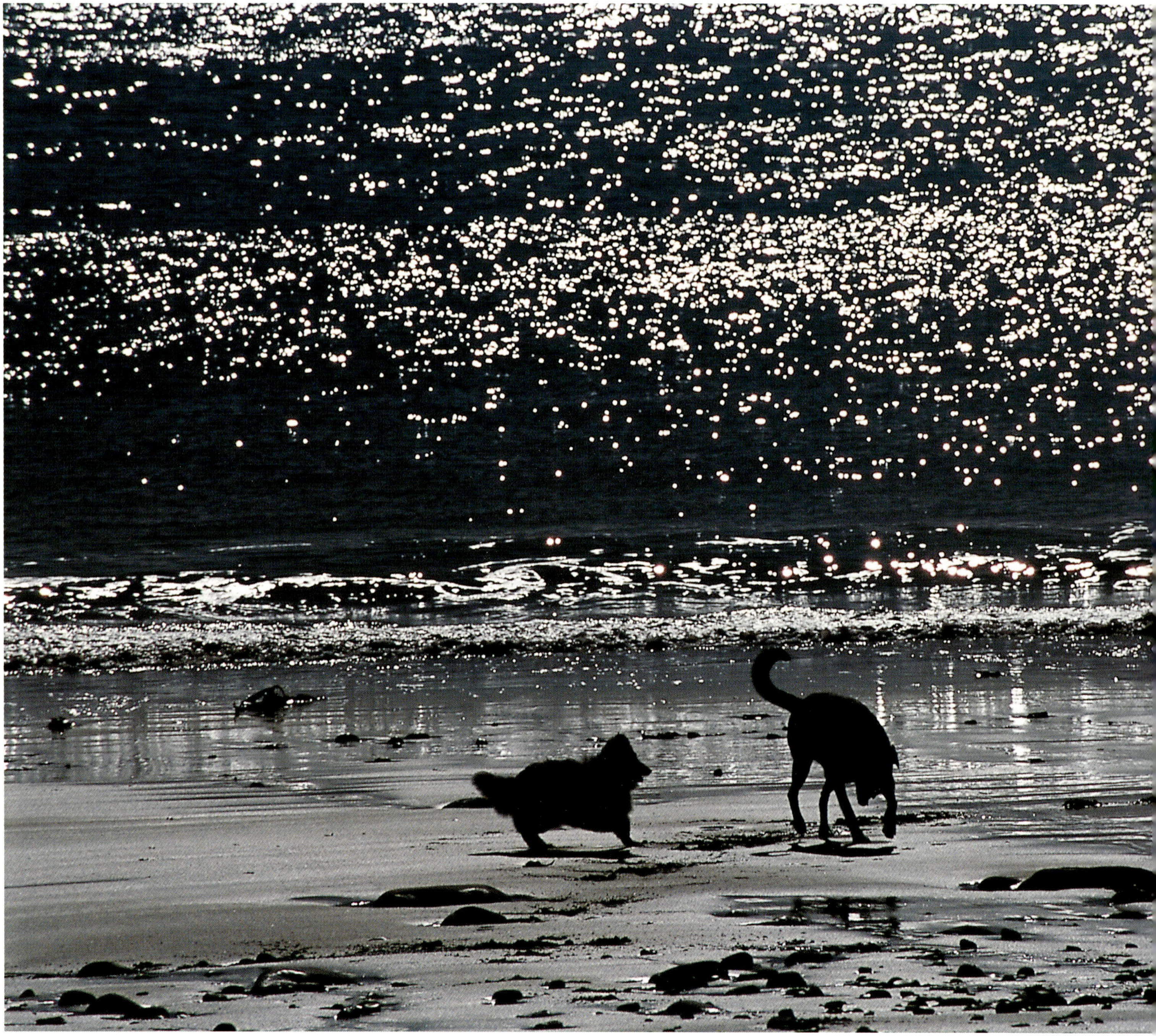

Zack and Fleck

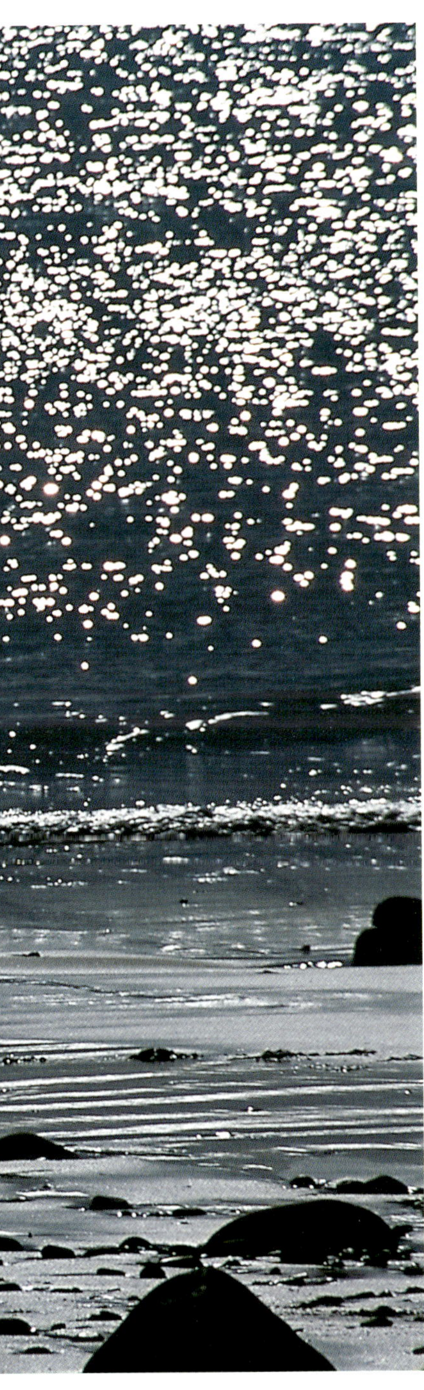

oh Happy Days

By Vanessa Giacopelli

St George's

Oh happy days, oh happy days...
When we used to pass the time away
Walking the dogs along the bay and throwing
them sticks .we used to play-
Carefree and fun the times we had
Along the bay with mum and dad.
The water glistened as the sun went away
I hope it'll still be here when I'm old and grey.
Take care of this beautiful bay –
I want to come back here with my kids one day,
Oh happy days!

Untitled

By Polly Crafter
Grainville

The dusk starts to settle,
The fog closes in.
My light shines so brightly,
The dark'll never win.

I'm surrounded by the water,
The street lamp shines my way.
I've seen so much history in my life,
Of words I cannot say.

I gaze across the water,
The castle I can see.
People visit her all day,
But no one visits me.

I stand and watch everything,
The shining castle does fade.
The night air's closing upon everything.
The long winding road I shade.

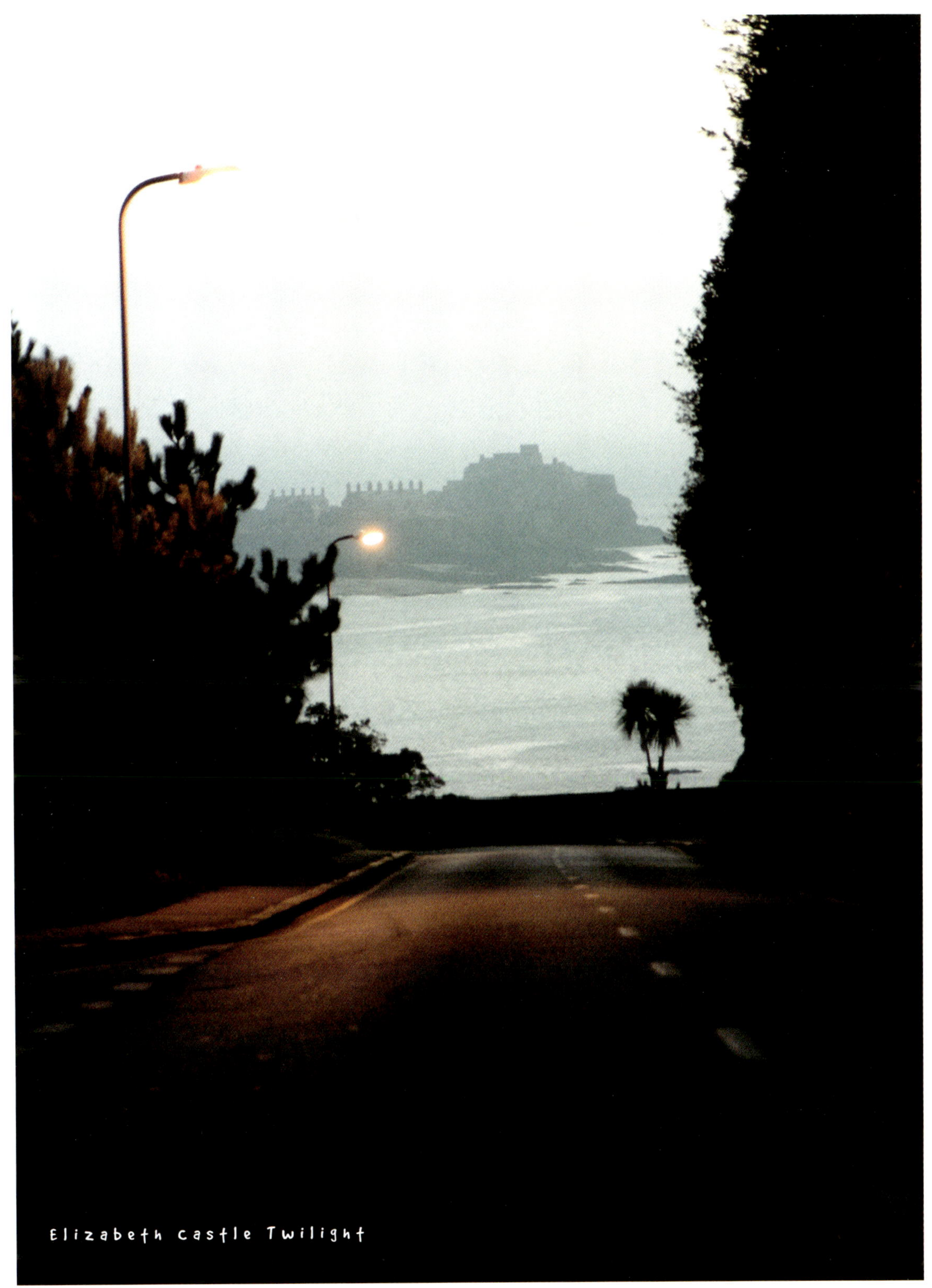

Elizabeth Castle Twilight

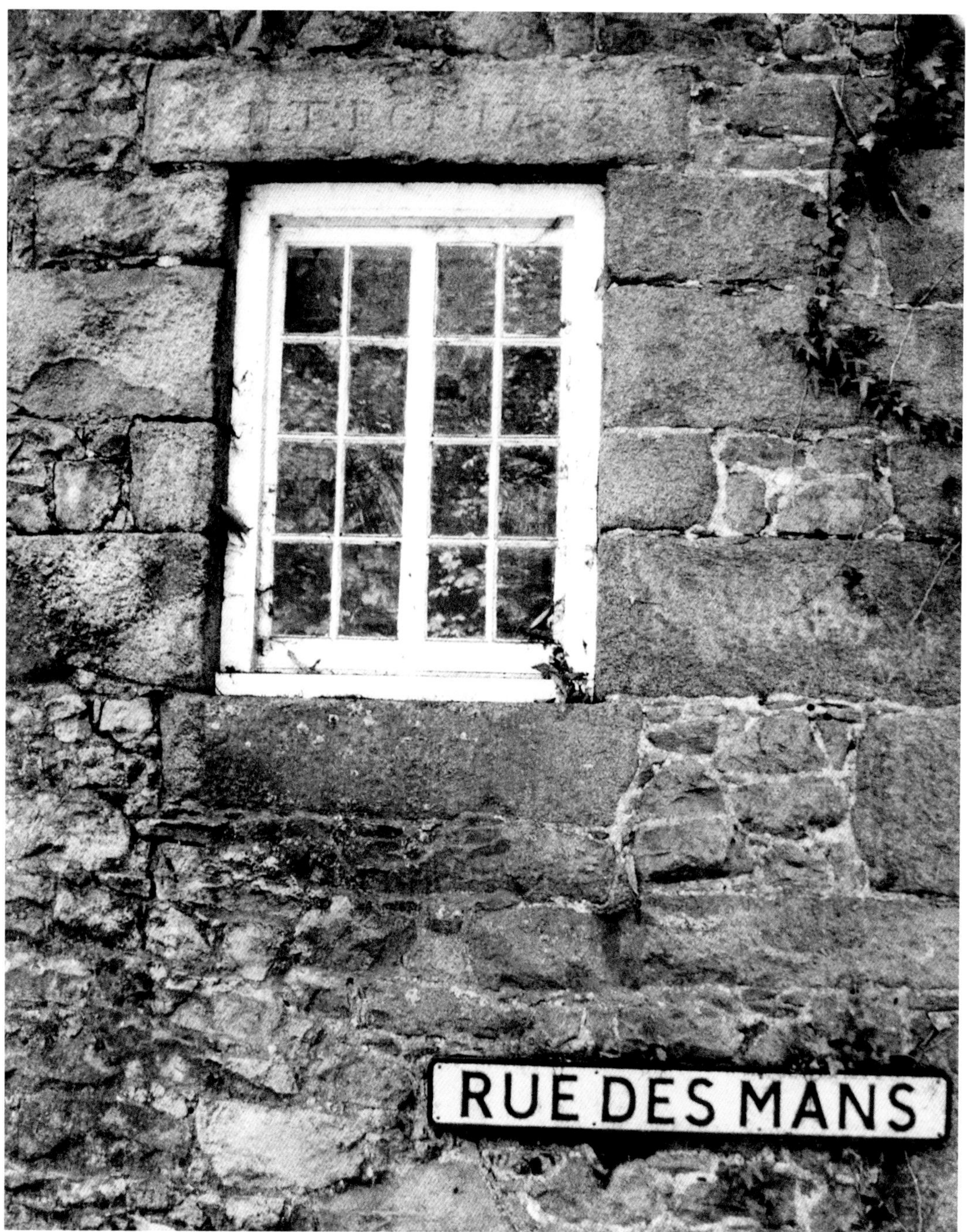

Rue des Mans

Untitled

By Louisa Crafter

Le Rocquier

Autumn browns, Dusty Greys,
Lack of colour cannot hide,
And a window, slowly rusting,
And the mysteries inside.

'Rue des Mans' proudly pinned,
Like a broach upon a coat.
Branch of ivy, decoration,
Like a flourish on a note.

Cosy home, stately house,
Falling into disrepair,
Crack in window, rust on taps
And a rotting wooden stair.

Granite cold, steely grey
Granite warm and leafy brown
Granite strong and smooth and regal
Wearing ivy like a gown.

Window

By Cassie Herdman

Le Rocquier

Window, window, on the wall
Window, window, seen it all
Window, window, what you see
Window, window, please tell me
Window, window, how you stare
Window, window, what's in there
Window, window, seen it all
Window, window, on the wall.

The Lookout Post

By Stephanie Sanderson
Haute Valleé

It once stood proud and strong,
Protecting the island from enemies that have come and gone.
With a view of the sea from miles around,
A place now where there is no sound
Except for bird song and the odd passers-by,
Left to ruins as time goes by.
It is now a place for thought, to think about the day,
It still stands proud and strong with nothing more to say.

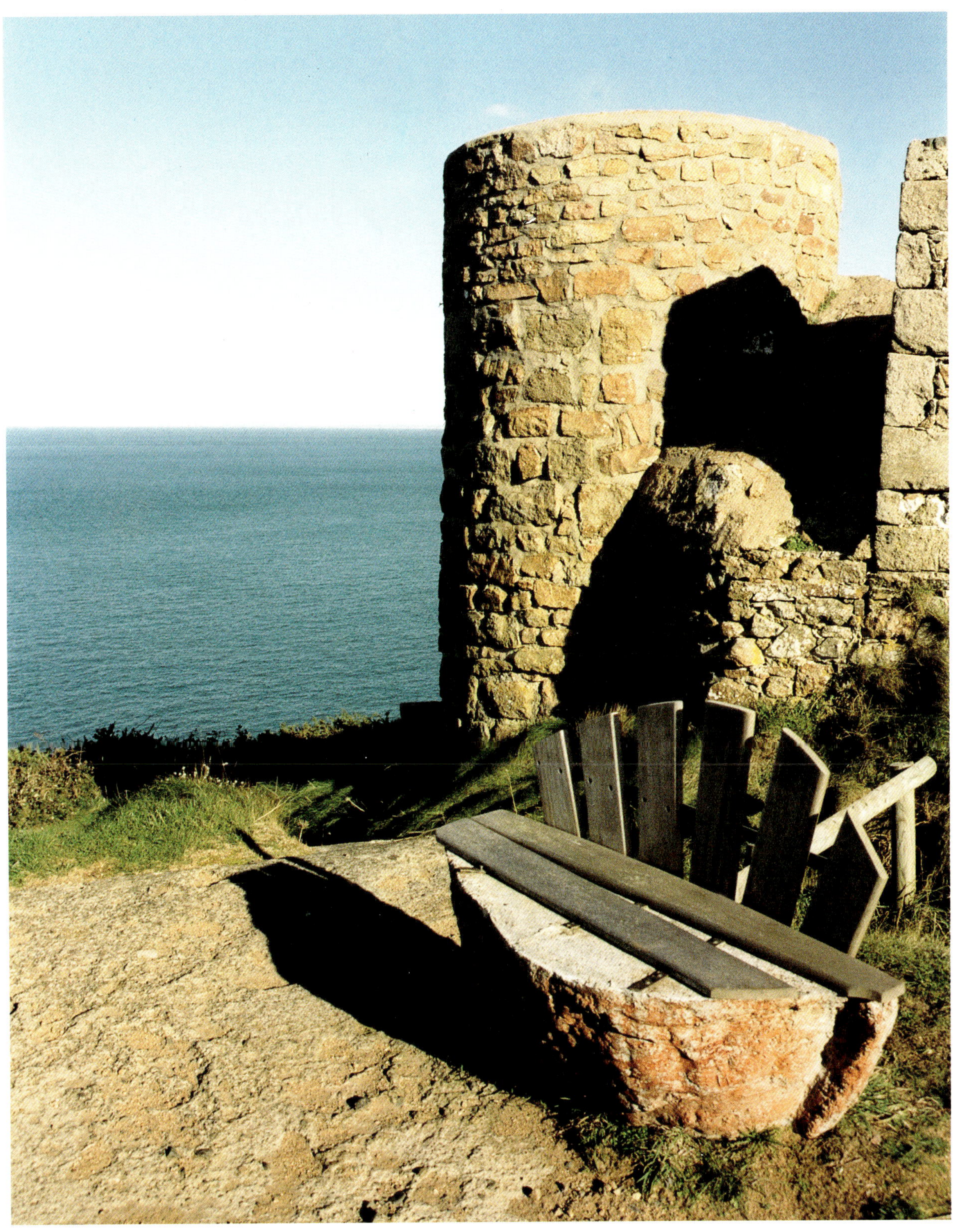

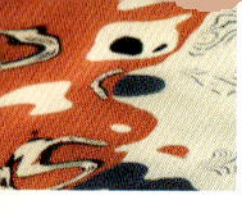

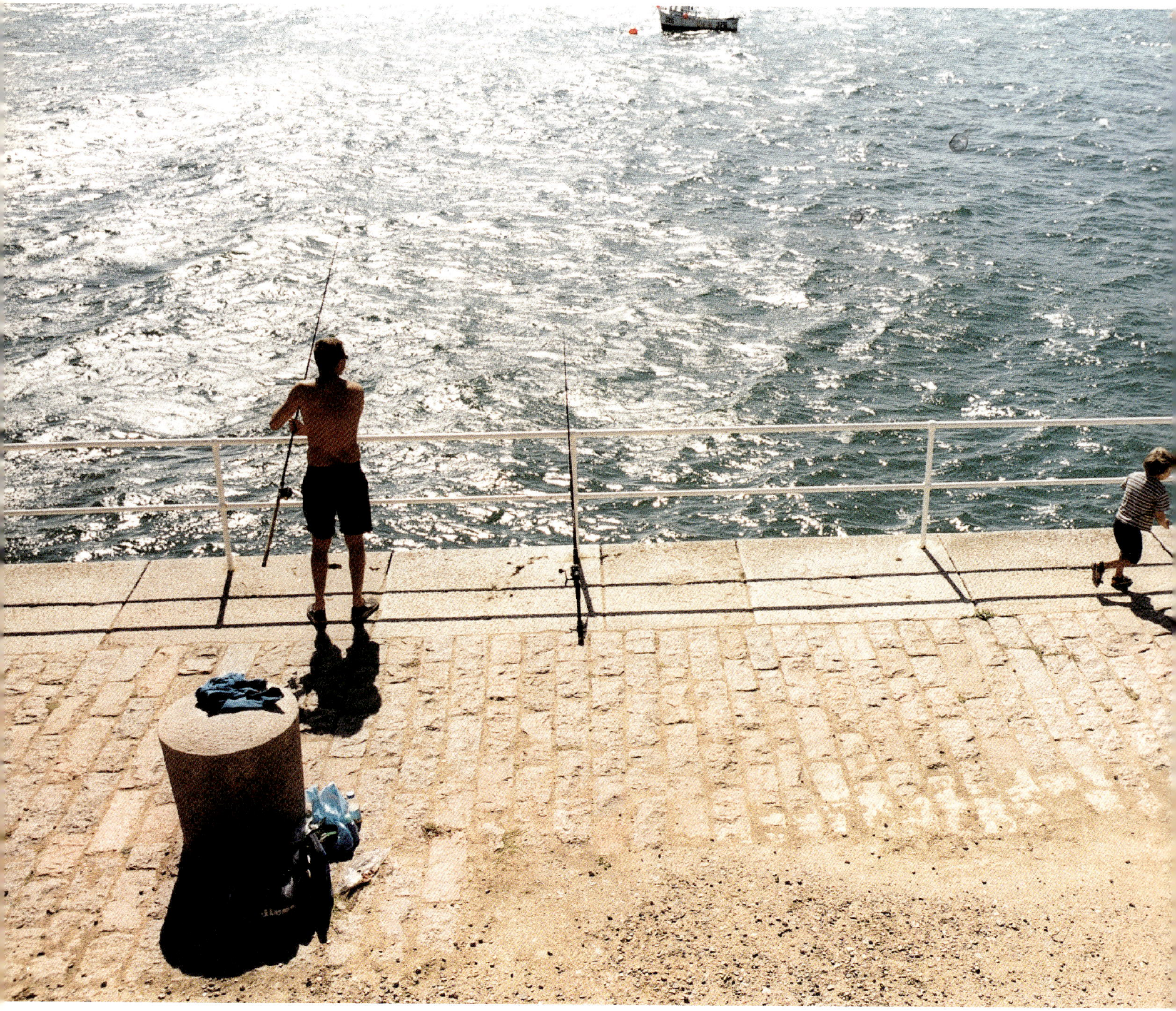

Fishing, St Catherine's

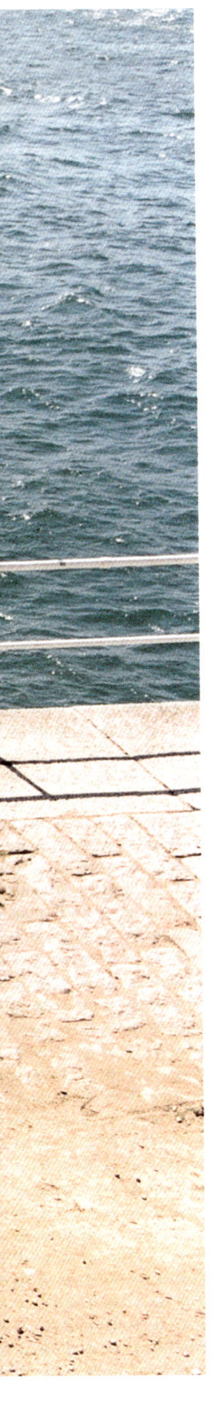

At the Breakwater

By Vicky Brady

Beaulieu

As the heat of the afternoon sun
Shines on the edge of the breakwater,
The clear, turquoise glimmer of the sea
Reflects the fisherman with his young helper.

The minds of the man and boy are clear as ice.
The stillness seems they are alone
The silence seems they are deep in thought
What could they be thinking about?

They see a fishing boat in the distance,
It sits on the surface of the sea.
It moves with the movement of the waves
And the sea sounds so soft and serene.

The anxious fisherman waits to catch his bait
The young boy has had enough.
The hands of the fisherman begin to ache
Until he finally catches what he wants.

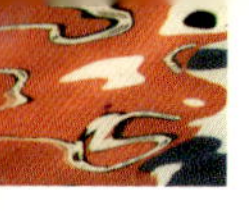

A crystal in the Universe's crown

By Lara Crenan and Helen Sandeman

Beaulieu

The darkness creeps over the light,
It is dusk, but soon night.
The earth will be covered in a blanket of purple,
Except when the moon shines in its own circle.

But the twinkling moon
Still sparkles and shines,
Like a crystal in the universe's crown.

The silhouettes of the buildings beneath the hill
Sit and sleep until morning is still.

The sea gently sways from side to side
With the moon's reflection stretching out beyond
the unseen sand,
At peace with the land.

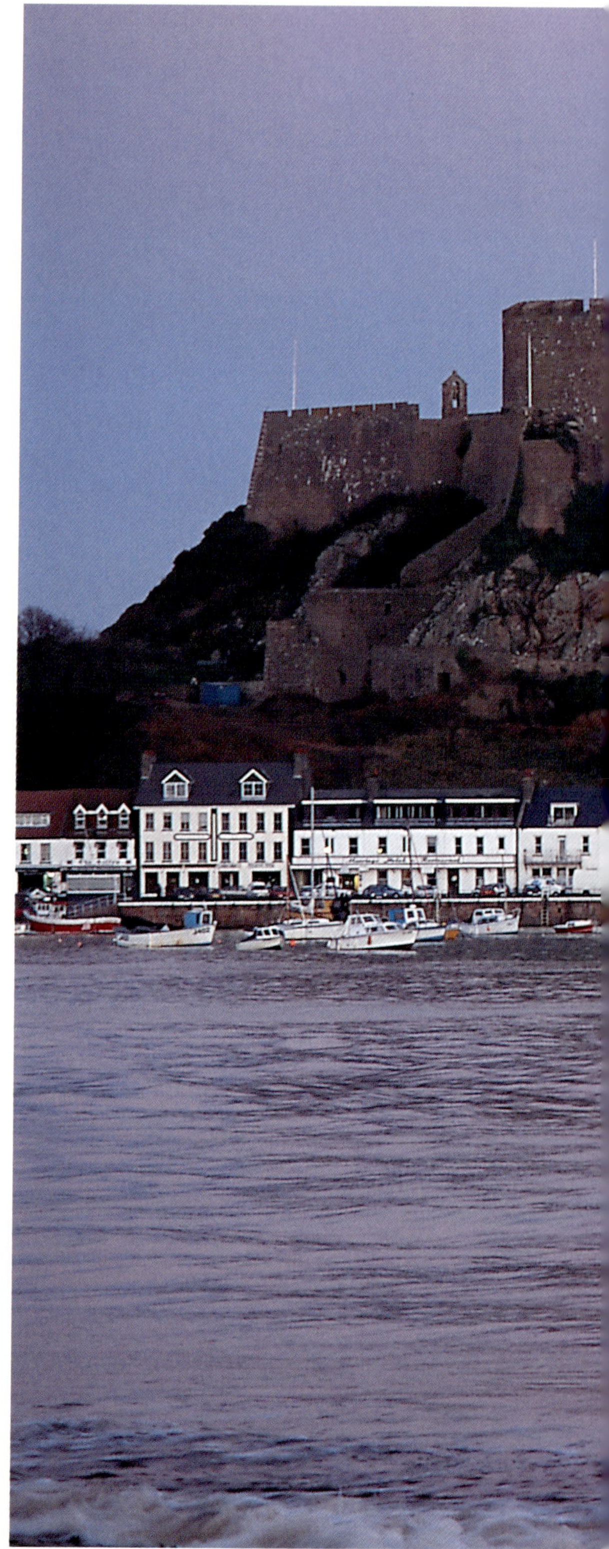

Gorey Moonlight

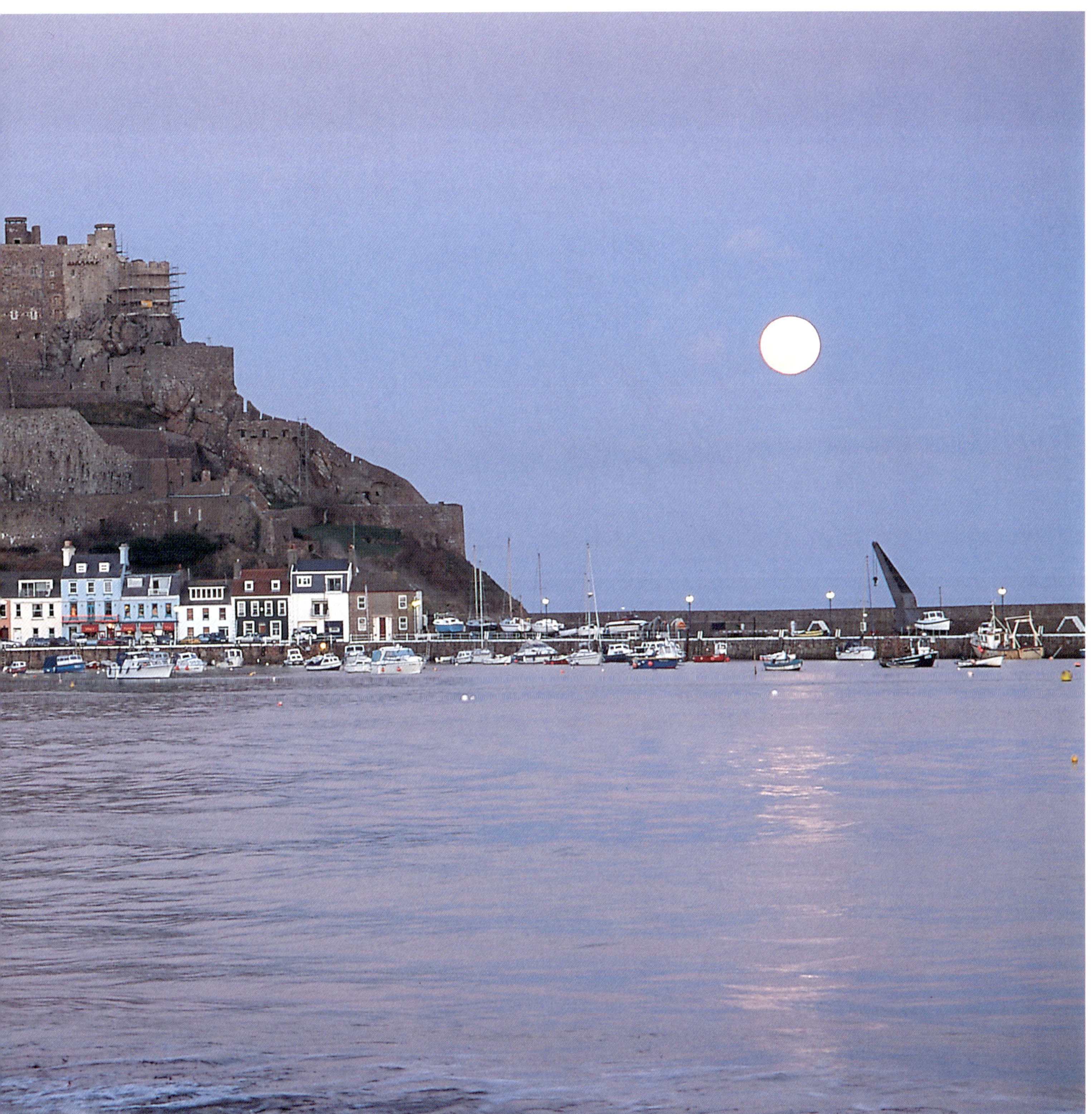

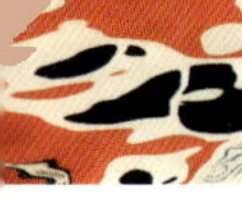

Lobster Pot

By Jason Fox
Le Rocquier

I'm lying on the shore,
Waiting to be seen.
Hoping to be used again,
By another Jersey Bean!

I'm very old and worn,
I've been used many times before.
Someday hopefully, my time will come,
To be used, many times more.

I have fed lots of people,
I hope to feed some more.
Catching what I can,
That come swimming up the shore.

I think my time is over now,
I'm too tired to carry on.
I'll have a rest, in the sun,
All my strength is gone.

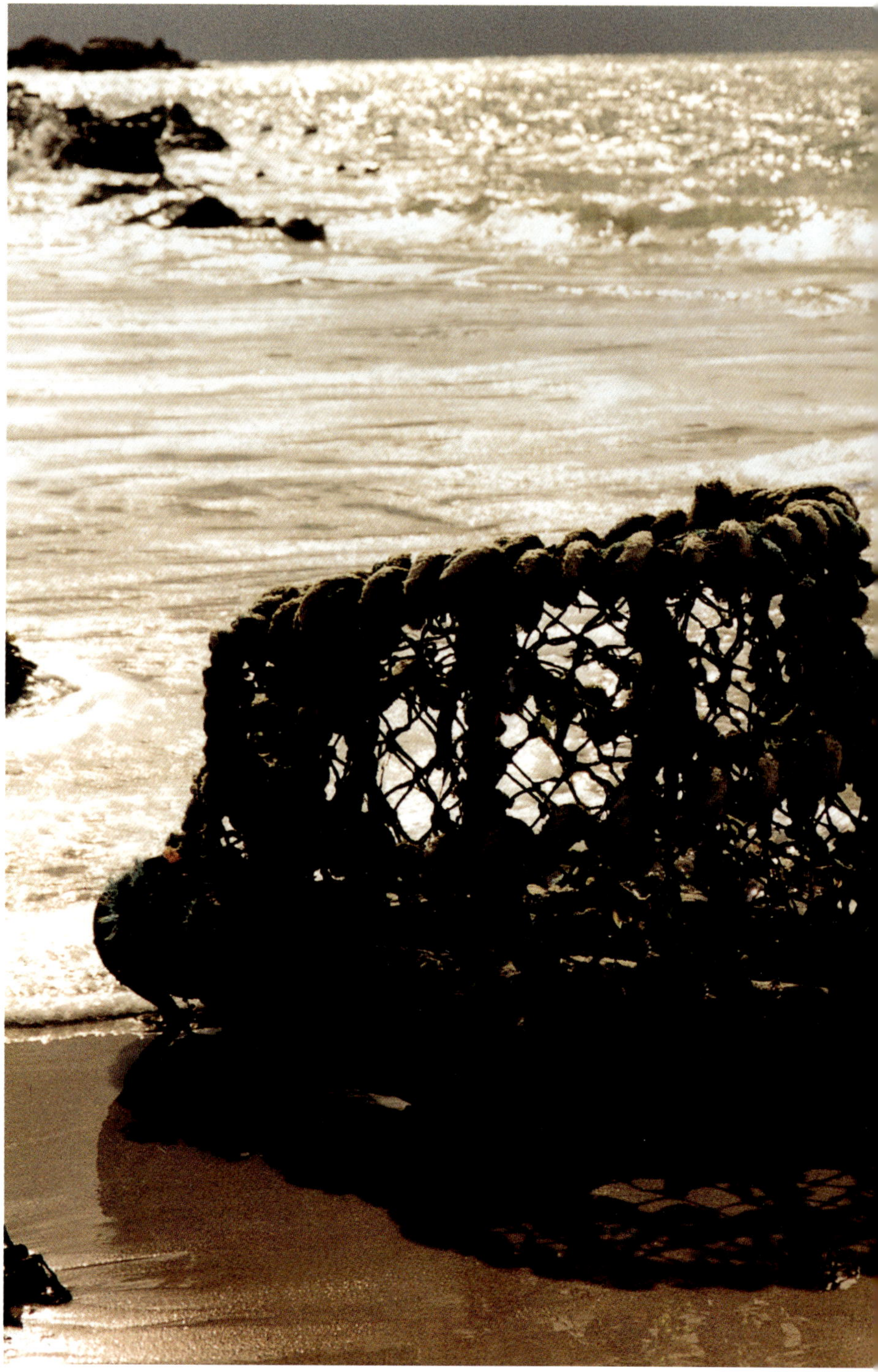

Lobster Pot

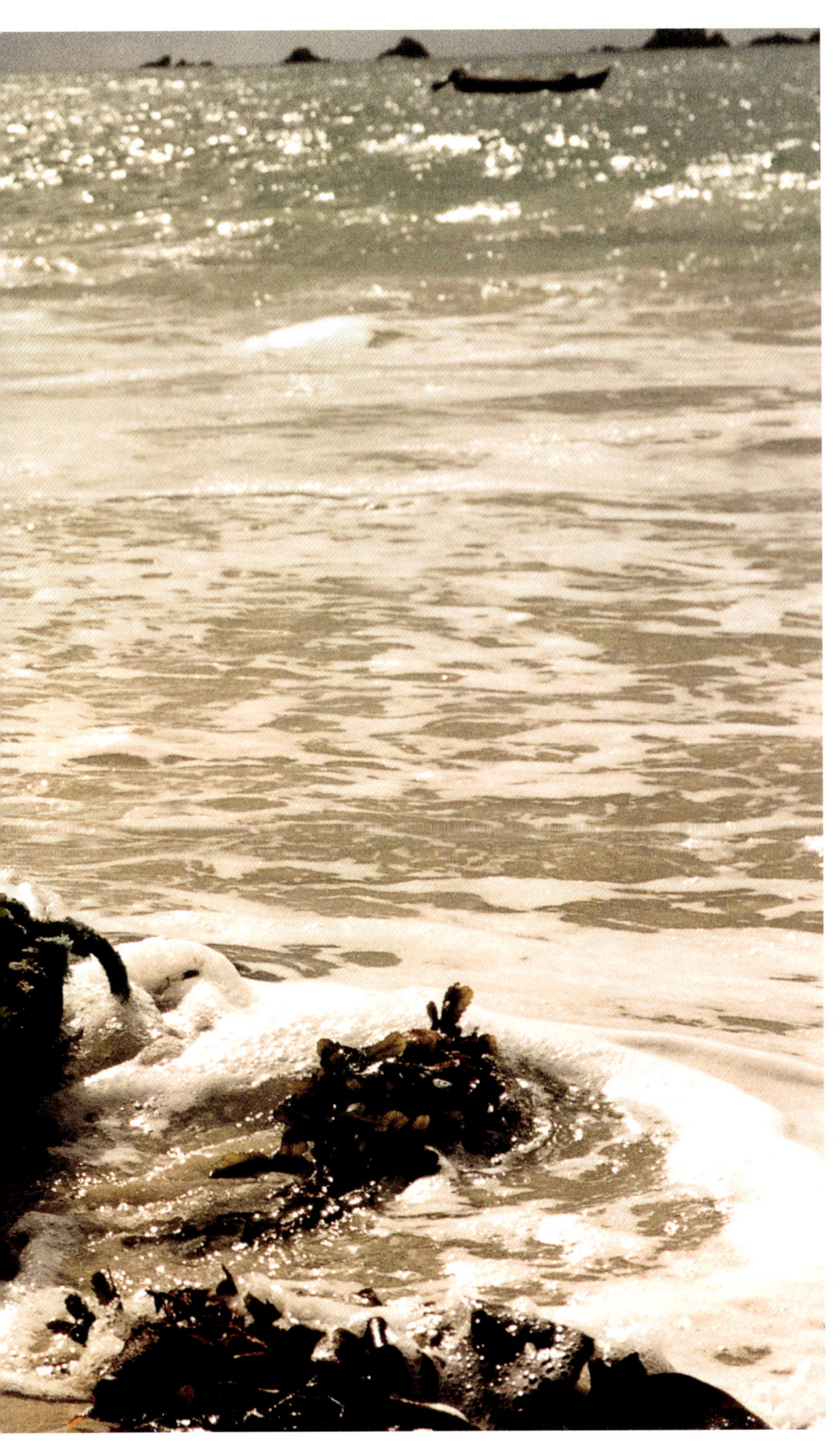

Forgotten

By Ross McCall

Victoria College

Alone
Left to rot
Decrepit
Falling to bits.

Disintegrating
Soon to go
Covered
Covered in seaweed.

Abandoned
No longer needed
Cast off
Expected to go.

To go
To go into nothing
Disappear
To never be seen again.

'Tis me the lobster pot sitting
On the barren beach as my lifetime expires
Twas me who was Rejected
'Tis me who is forgotten
'Tis me
'Tis me the lobster pot...

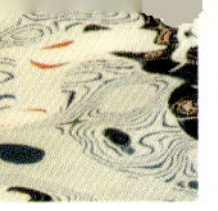

Beneath the old, old Tree

By Amelia Churchill Blackie
St George's

The Sun's gleaming rays
awoke the morning
smiling down upon the woods.
The daffodils opened their eyes,
singing to the day,
chatting to the world.
Ladybirds,
Spiders,
tiptoe across diamonds of dew,
greeting everyone who passed.
At last the great, old tree
opened his droopy, sleepy eyes,
said "Good morning" to Nature,
in his low, hollow voice.

He had stood there for centuries,
with the breeze
ruffling his leaves,
and creaking limbs,
this way,
and that,
watching seeds grow into flowers,
and flowers into seeds.
He was wise,
knowing of every living thing.
He was everybody's friend,
and everybody's home.
And when the Sun goes in,
all the flowers bow their heads,
taking shelter for the night,
beneath the old, old tree.

Spring, St Brelade

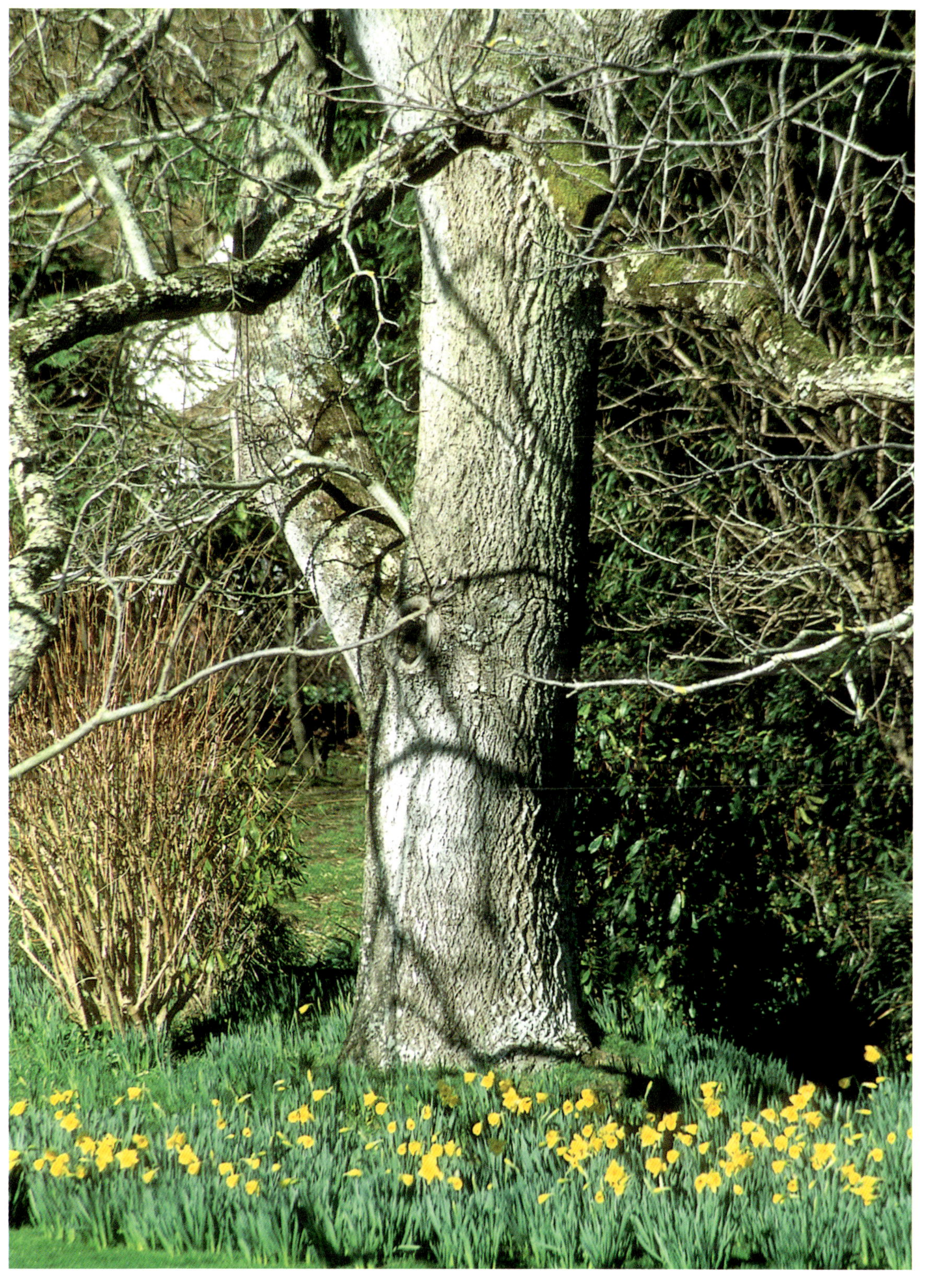

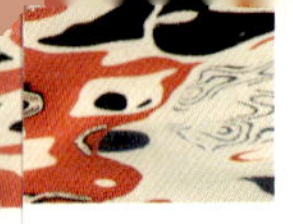

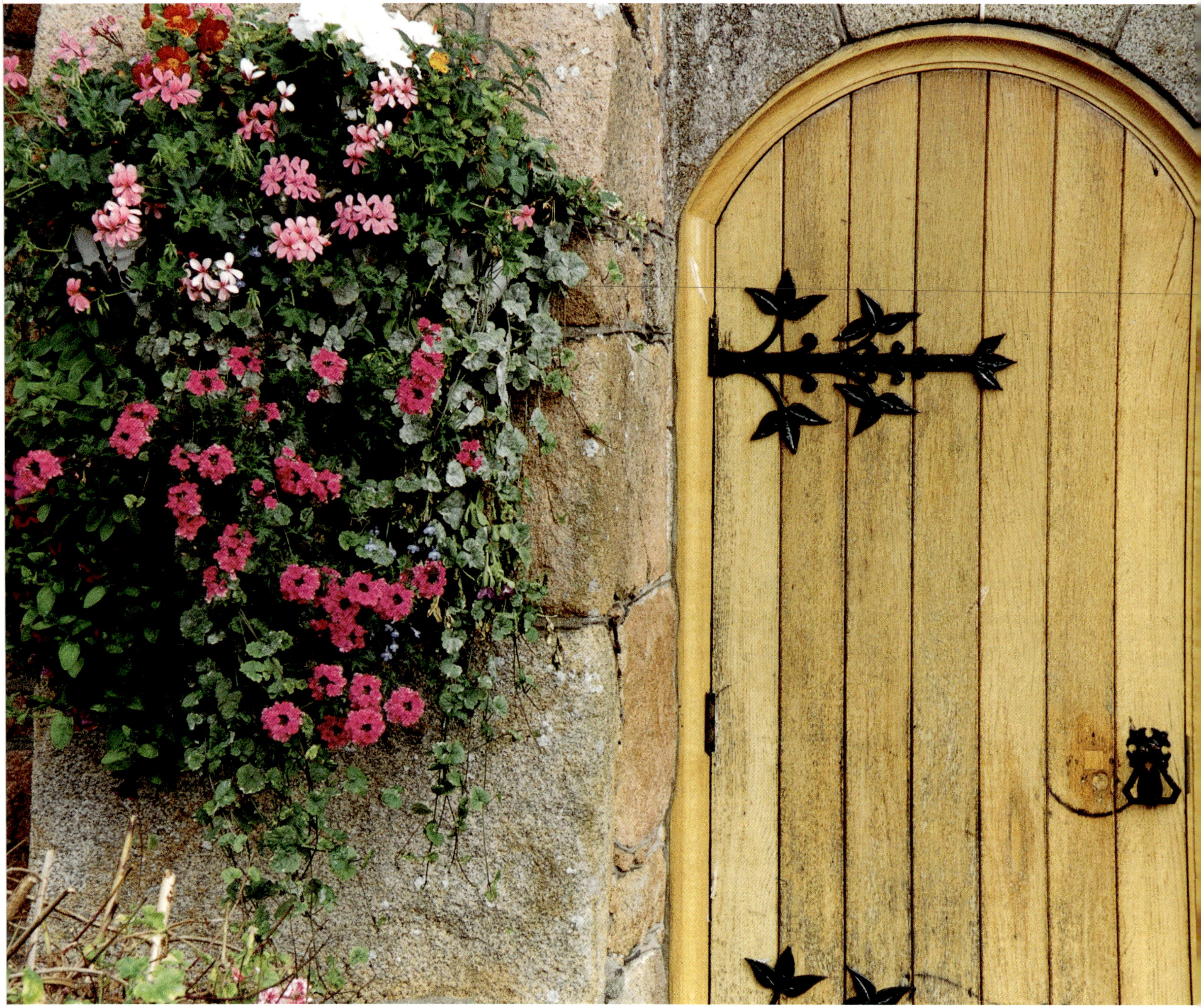

The Door

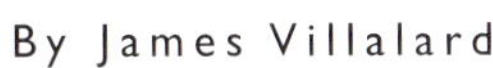

By James Villalard

De La Salle

Portals to another world,
Bolted or open wide,
Concealing events within,
Or inviting us inside.

Love-rats forget to lock them,
So they're always found,
Flirting with the neighbour's spouse,
Rolling on the ground.

They are a part of every house,
But it's rather hard,
Getting in without a key,
Because they're locked and barred.

The Door

By Timothy Faudemer

De La Salle

What lies beneath this closed door?
Are things beyond good and well?
As the figure of this great bold door,
Means we can never see to tell.

Do deathly murderers lie beyond?
Or possibly angels on a mission,
Are people of their friends so fond?
It all boils down to an inaccurate superstition.

The truth is we will never know,
Unless we open this closed door,
So let's confront our fears and foe,
And open up this door.

Because life's got many doors,
And through them we must wander,
Its one of life's many laws,
So let's move on, not ponder.

The Waves

By Angharad Mallon
Les Quennevais

The waves are shiny,
As shimmering pennies on dull pavements.

The sun beams on waves,
As child's faces beam at sight of ice creams.

The spray goes as high,
As birds flying to the sky.

The waves look as wild,
As vicious cheaters chasing prey.

The waves contain many shades,
As the rainbow contains colours.

The spray's as free,
As a child running through a field of daisies.

The delicate wave licks the wall with its lacy tongue
The silky waves lap against each other in a random motion.

THE WAVES ARE ALIVE

Gorey Pier

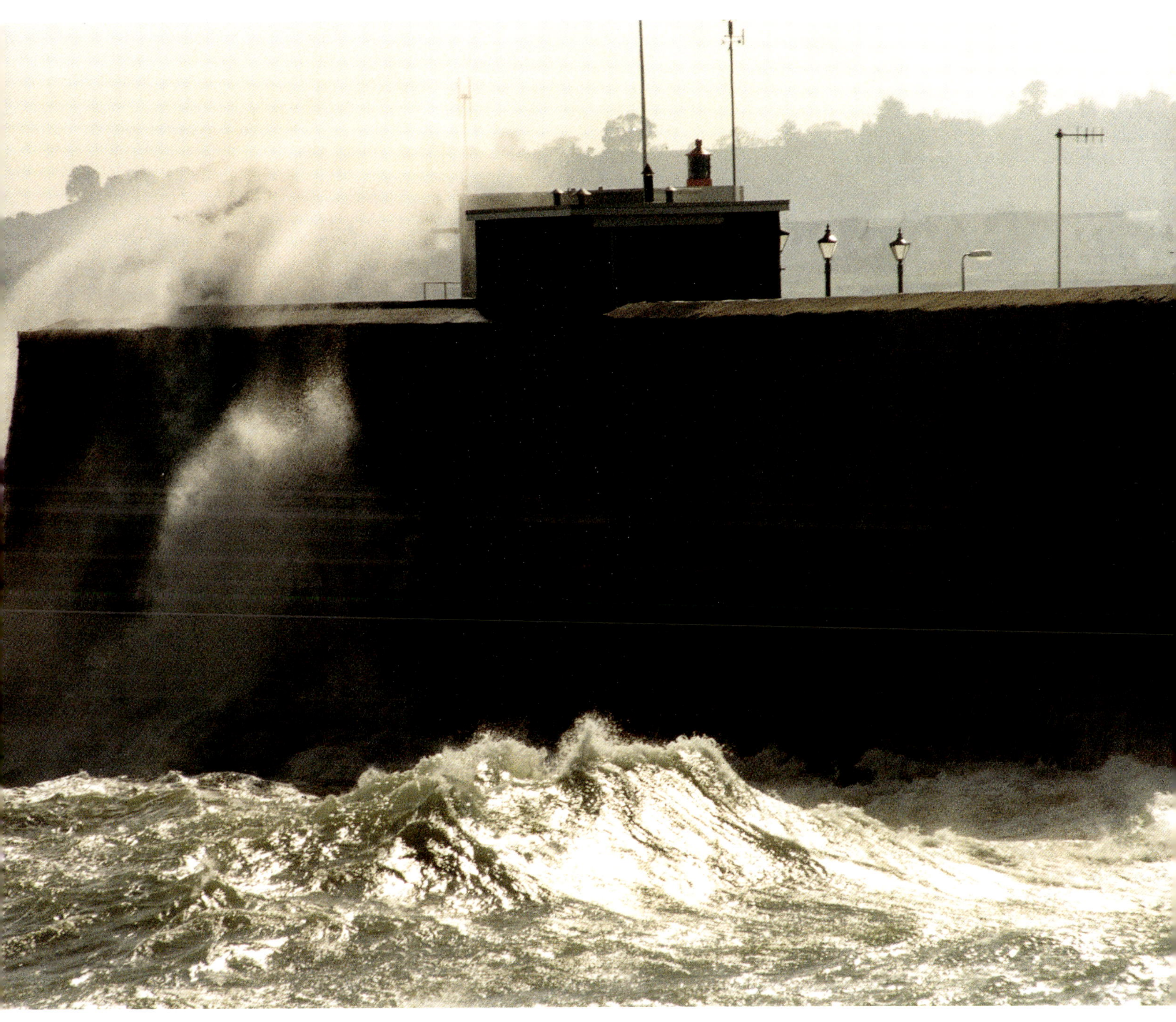

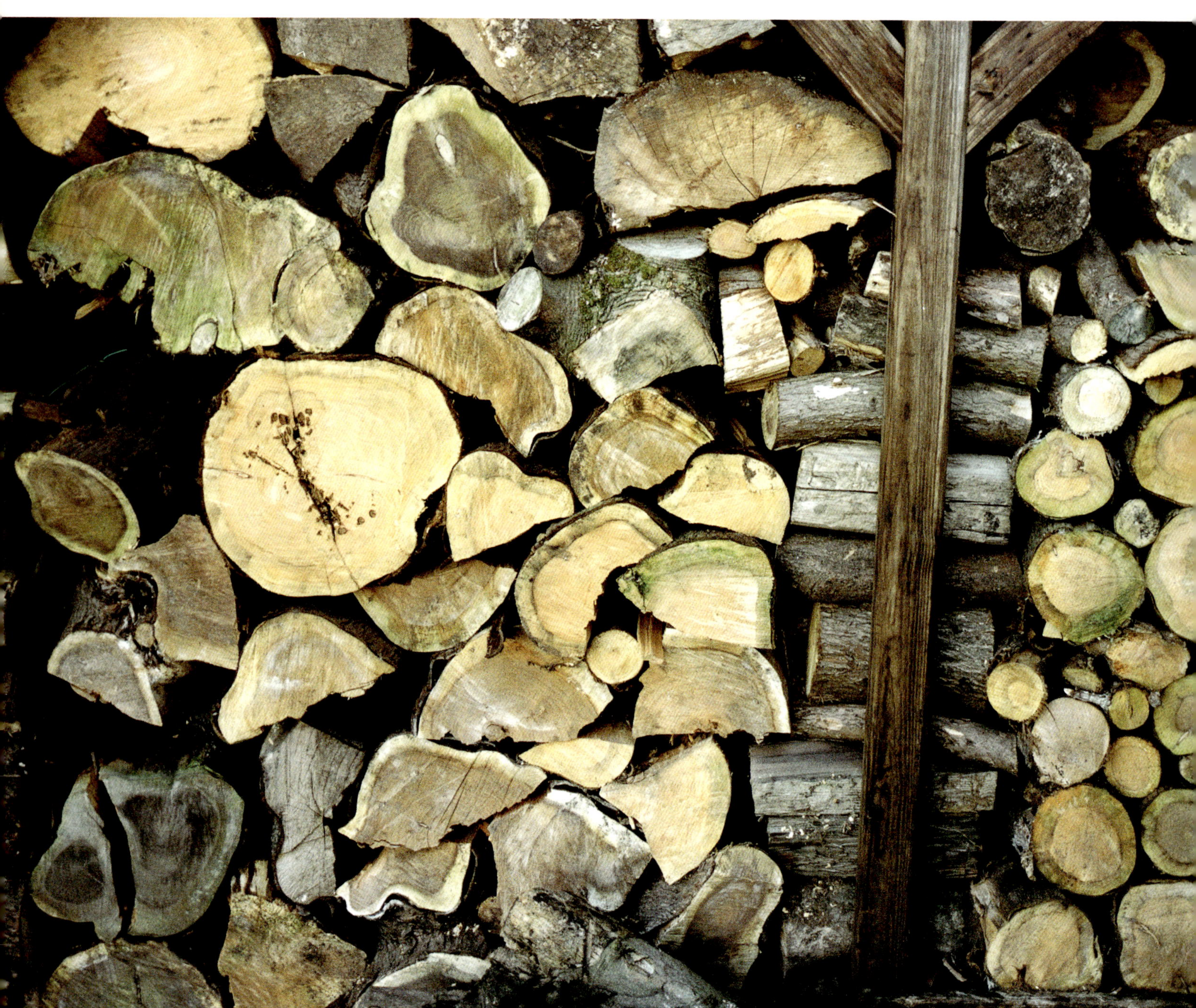

Stacked for Winter

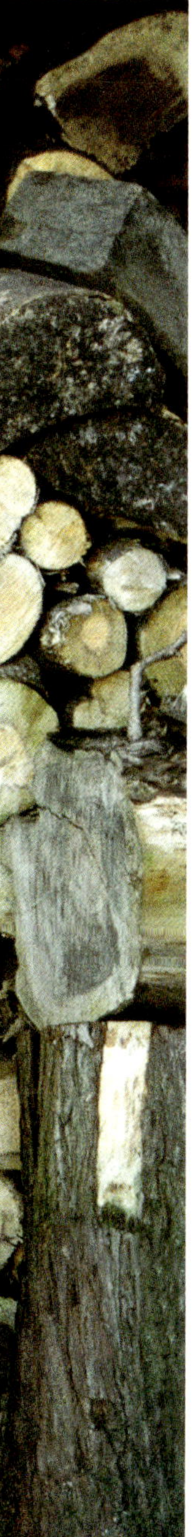

Cut Down

Sophie Taylor

Jersey College for Girls

As Autumn slowly turns to Winter
Dragging its cold, snow coat,
The cabin dwellers bring in the fallen
logs of old
To burn brightly, warming the bodies inside.
The pile of wood builds up and up
As the leaves turn gold and are swept away.

Where do they come from these
statues of the land?
Where will they go?

The weather turns cold and bitter
The frost gets worse and worse
And gradually more trees are cut down
Still in their prime of life
As we use and bruise the planet around us
So that we can be warm and bright.

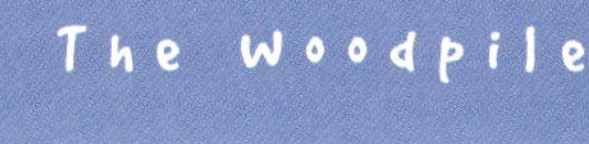

The Woodpile

By Mel Boléat

Hautlieu

So many faces, people all together,
Marching down the street,
They resemble logs,
Packed close together, overpopulated.

Folk age, whilst trees gain rings,
Both have observed many things,
From a distance and up close,
Although some don't tell.

The fading language, Jersey French,
Is hanging like a withered branch,
Soon to be lost forever,
Chopped down and cast aside.

Handsome granite buildings are still standing,
Enlightening us about the past,
The trees remain around them,
Still there, still proud.

Masses of new homes are built,
In the town and country,
Trees are planted, too,
Never forgotten.

As Jersey fills up like a log shed,
We must stop and think.
We don't want our lovely island spoilt,
We want Jersey's beauty to live on,
Just like the trees.

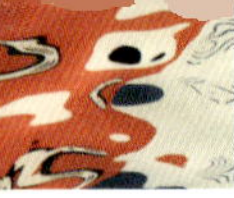

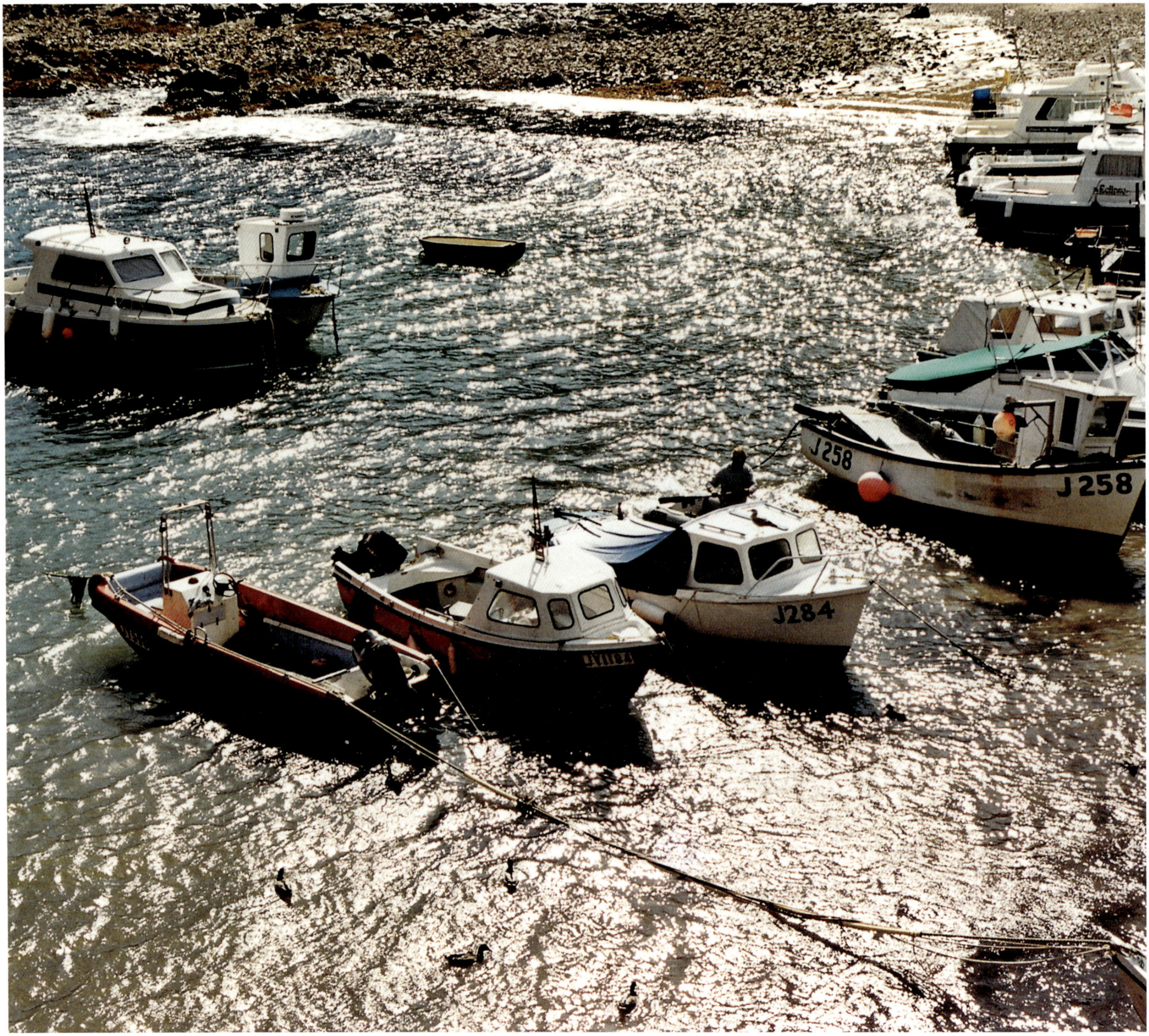

Bonne Nuit

Glory of the Sea.

By Carla Jardim
Haute Valleé

The mist of the night fades and the Sun rises,
As usual.
Gracing Bonne Nuit Bay with his tender smile.
The worries, troubles and high tide of the night
slowly recede, leaving only high hopes for today
and a gentle warmth, to bring a smile to my
weathered face.
As the sea shimmers and sparkles irridescently
around me and the gulls, call out desolately overhead,
the traders begin.
Opening the cafes, shops and stalls, life continues as it
has for so long. The tourists come, laughing. chattering
amongst themselves,
so clearly amused at our quaint, subdued life.
A world away from their own.
We watch the other boats put out to sea, their
owners contented, and as they do, my
reminiscing begins.
I remember the days when I, too, was
one of them.
Of when I, too, breathed the salt sea air. Swam,
swam lithe and free as a wild dolphin,
with the wind at my back and a song in my heart.
Carelessly plucking the fruits of the sea.
Stealing them away from her, from under her nose,
while she hurried me back to shore with a swish of
her gossamer gown.
Back to those on shore,
those who had never truly lived.
Who would share their brief existence with her, but
never fully know her.
Her power, her many faces and moods,
her depth and her clarity.
I am now no longer part of her, one with her, just
another admirer.
Another who wishes that I could break free of
my mooring.
One whose forbearance can scarce hold
another day,
until I am restored to my former glory.
If only, I whisper mournfully.

But now once again, I roam, in the sea's loving arms
once more.
Plucking her fruits while she whispers in my ear.
To be respected by the sailor who aids me,
who sings, laughs and talks with me.
Admires my vivid new colours, who calls me by my
name, sees,
past my number to my heart and soul.
Shares my love of the sea,
and makes the old days seem monotonous
and pointless.
She who gave me my name, which I bear with
the utmost honour.
Glory of the Sea.
While I live, breathe and be.
Who I am.
Glory of the Sea.

A Peaceful Silence

By Alicia Biney
Grainville

A calming lake and a gentle breeze,
All the world seems at ease,
As the day moves out and the night moves in,
All the birds protect their kin.

Made to last, a paradise for all,
Nothing could make this empire fall,
A place for anyone to rest their eyes,
A home for pigeons and sparrows to rise.

A place for romance to blossom and grow,
A place we let our true feelings show,
Somewhere that only smiles will you find,
Something too special, to be wiped from your mind.

Where time stands still, and will wait for us all,
Where playing children hear their dear mother call,
A place that protects life in itself,
A place that is better than any man's wealth.

A place that will be there any time of the day, Somewhere
inside us, that will never fade away.

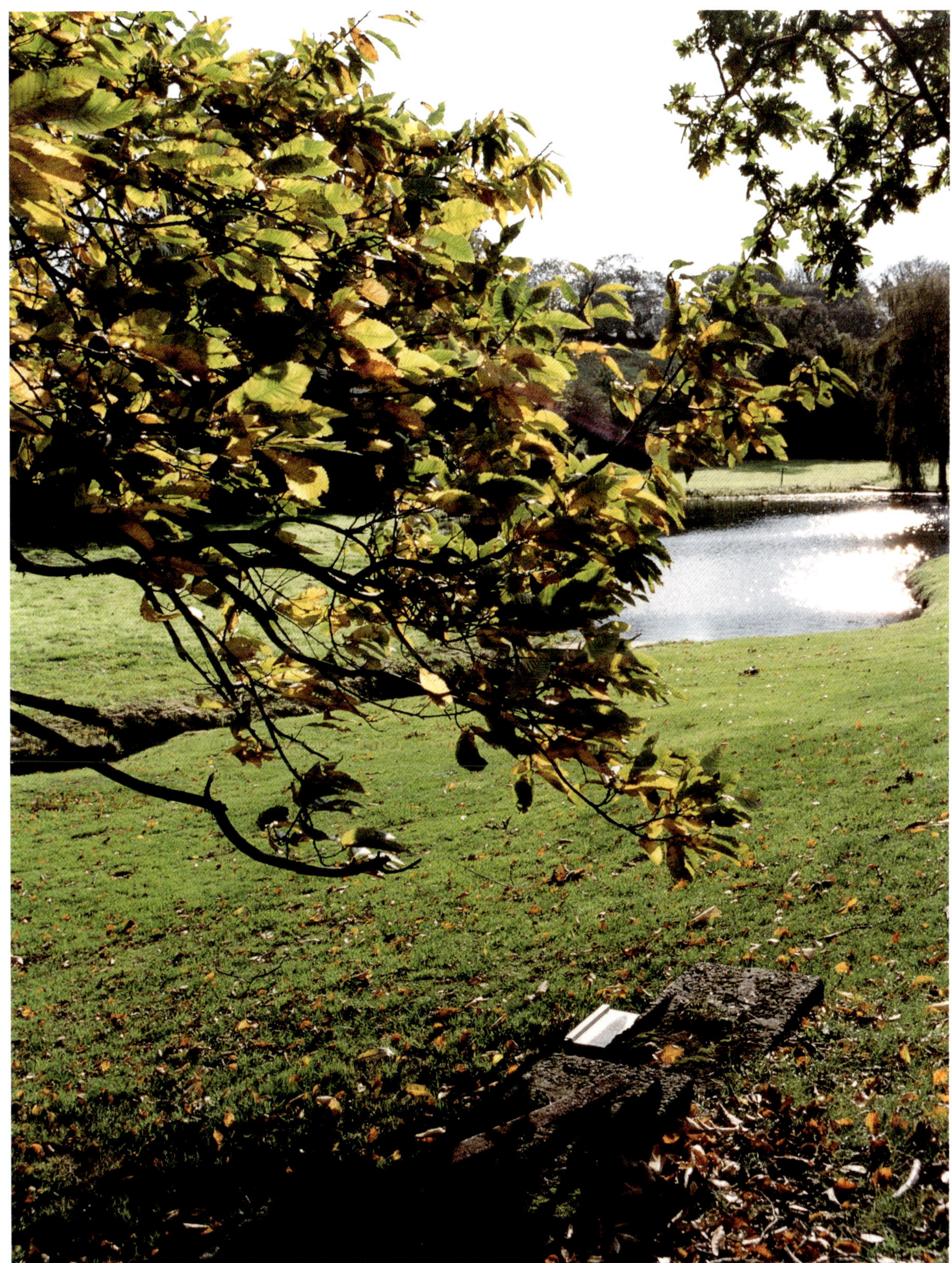

Valley

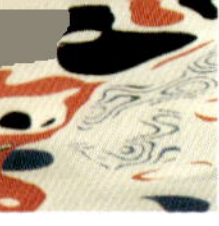

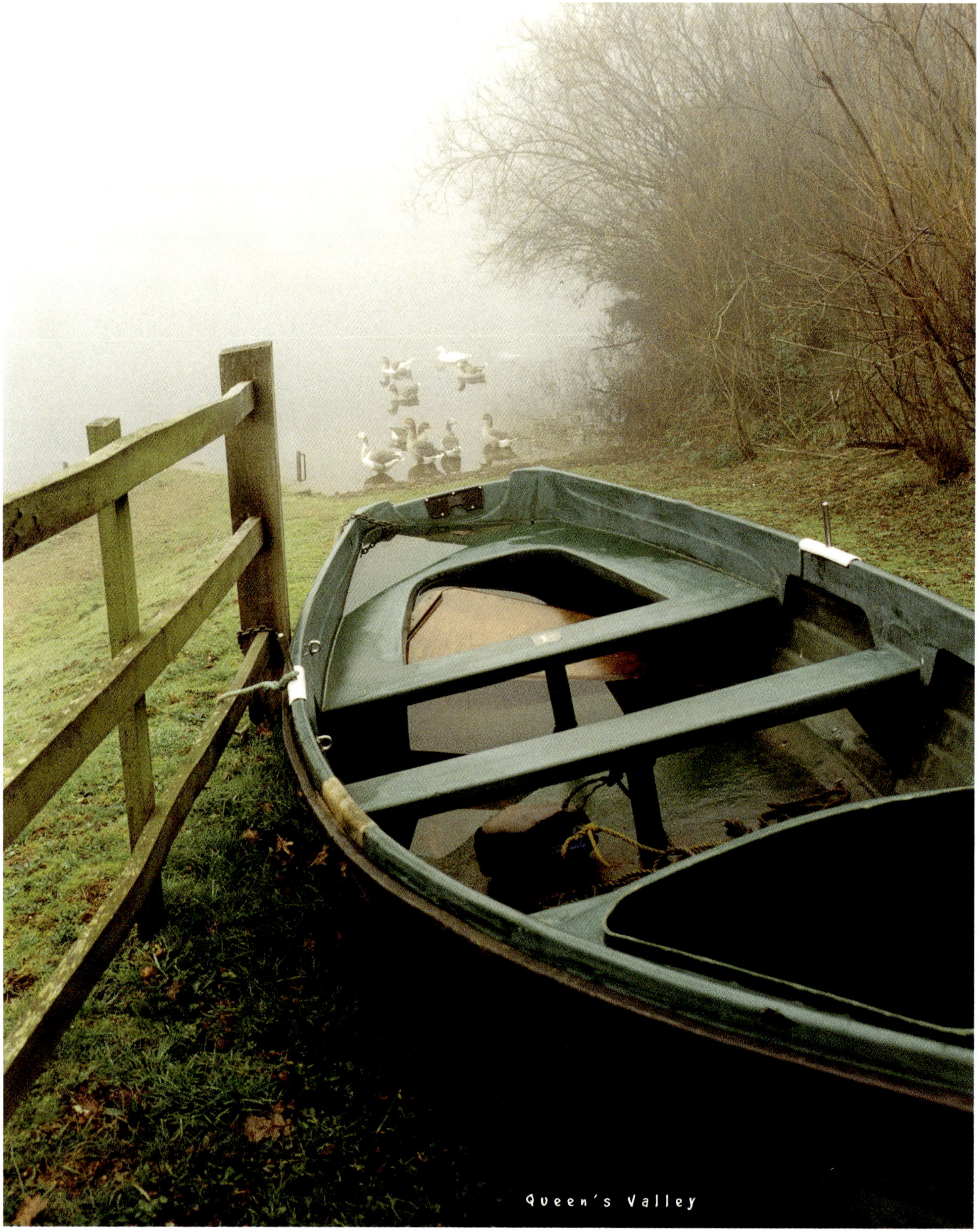

Queen's Valley

Misty Days

By Oliver Ireson

St George's

The misty clouds zoom in on to a little area as a flock of small ducks,
geese and seagulls fly over into a small peaceful lake.
A small, green rowing boat lies in a shadowy, overgrown patch of grass.
The trees flow in the direction of the soft blowing breeze.

The Misty Morning

By Oliver Weston

St George's

Through the early morning mist
stood a sage green rowing boat.
There was a gnarled tree stood to one side,
it stood bare; there were no leaves on its branch.
Through the mist there was a gleaming lake,
you could see the geese's reflection on the mirror like water.
The mist was creeping eerily round the lake
Standing there you felt like an evil spirit was cast over you,
a twig snapped; I whirled round. 'Is there a ghost?' I thought to myself.
I began to walk back through the damp grass.
Was there someone watching me?
I got back on to the path and turned
round to see the sinister scene once more.
I looked behind me again;
there was someone watching me, I thought.
I ran as fast as I could.
Was I going mad or was there really something wicked going on,
on that cold winter's morning?

Memories

By Ashley Le Hegarat

Les Quennevias

Lights burning away,
Fiercely in the distance.
Reflecting in the near water.
Clear water, surface calm, but currents drag
Restless ferries and boats back from the open sea.
I see the ferries and think of the past,
The happy, but alienated past.

The past is sad,
But strangely comforting.
Looking down on Elizabeth Port,
From Fort Regent's hill.
The light neon waters disturb memories,
Memories sunk deep by time.
The water slips between the ports,
Like the memories sinking deep in to my mind.

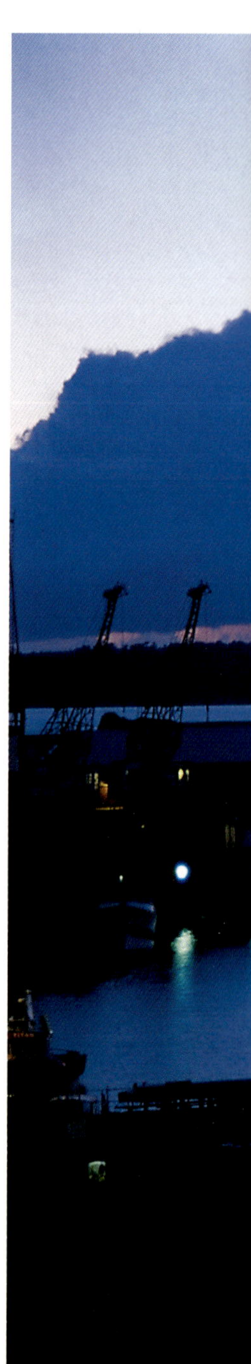

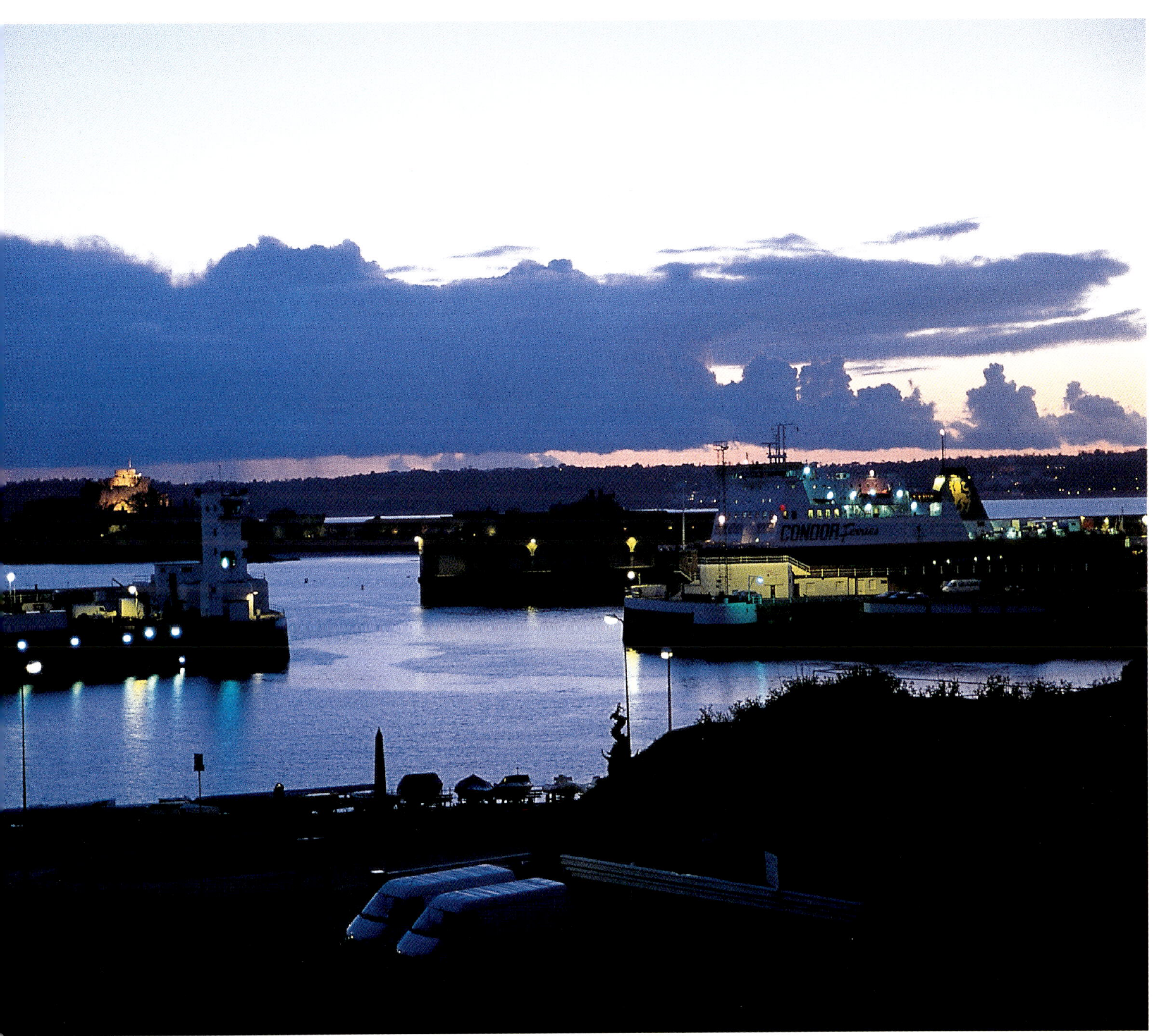

St Helier Harbour

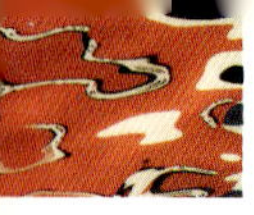

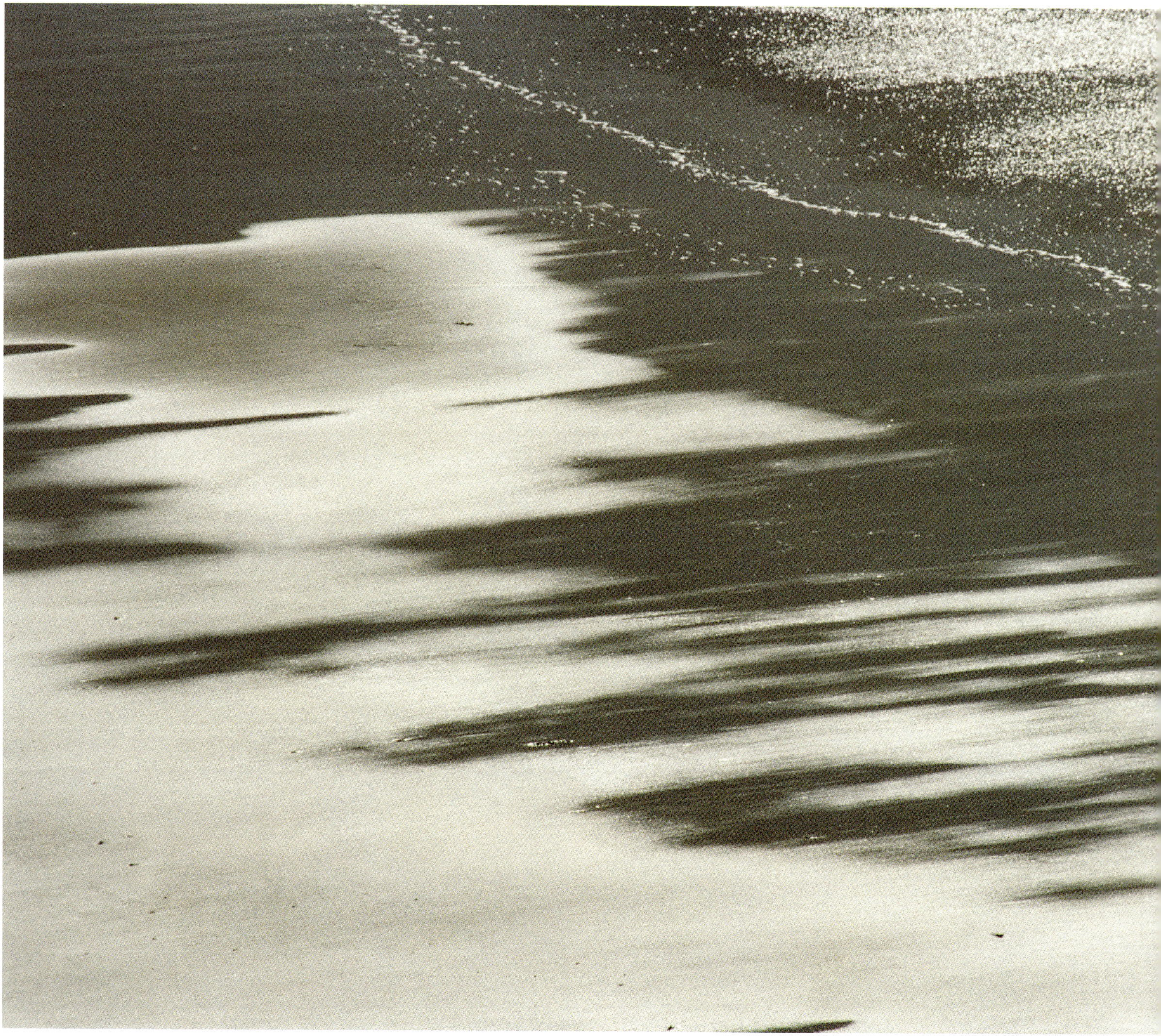

Ouaisne

Untitled

By Hannah Leech

Grainville

Walking on the beach
Feel the smooth sand underneath
Your feet.

The sea ripples between your toes,
As the tide ebbs.
The sun warms your face,
Eyes squinting in the sunlight,
Hair blowing in the breeze.
Wind howling in your ears,
Clouds rolling through the sky like cotton wool balls,
Feeling totally free
At peace with the world.

on the Beach.

By Nadine Martins

Haute Valleé

On the beach there's plenty to hear,
The seagulls, the sea, are all so near.
Kids are eating ice-creams with friends,
And smiling into the camera lens,
Underneath the blazing hot sun,
Enjoying the waves and the golden sand,
And lots of people, all trying to get tanned.
On the beach there's plenty to hear,
The seagulls, the sea, are all so near,
Kids are eating their ice-creams with friends,
And of course, all are smiling into the camera lens.

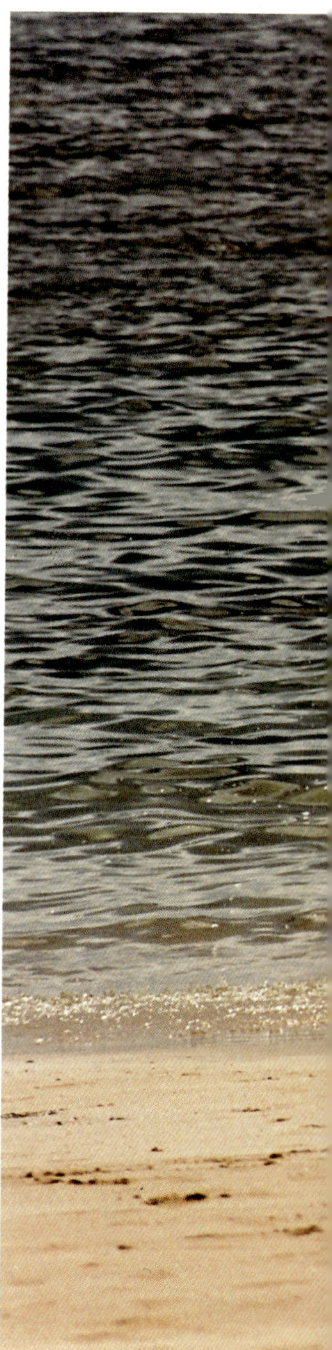

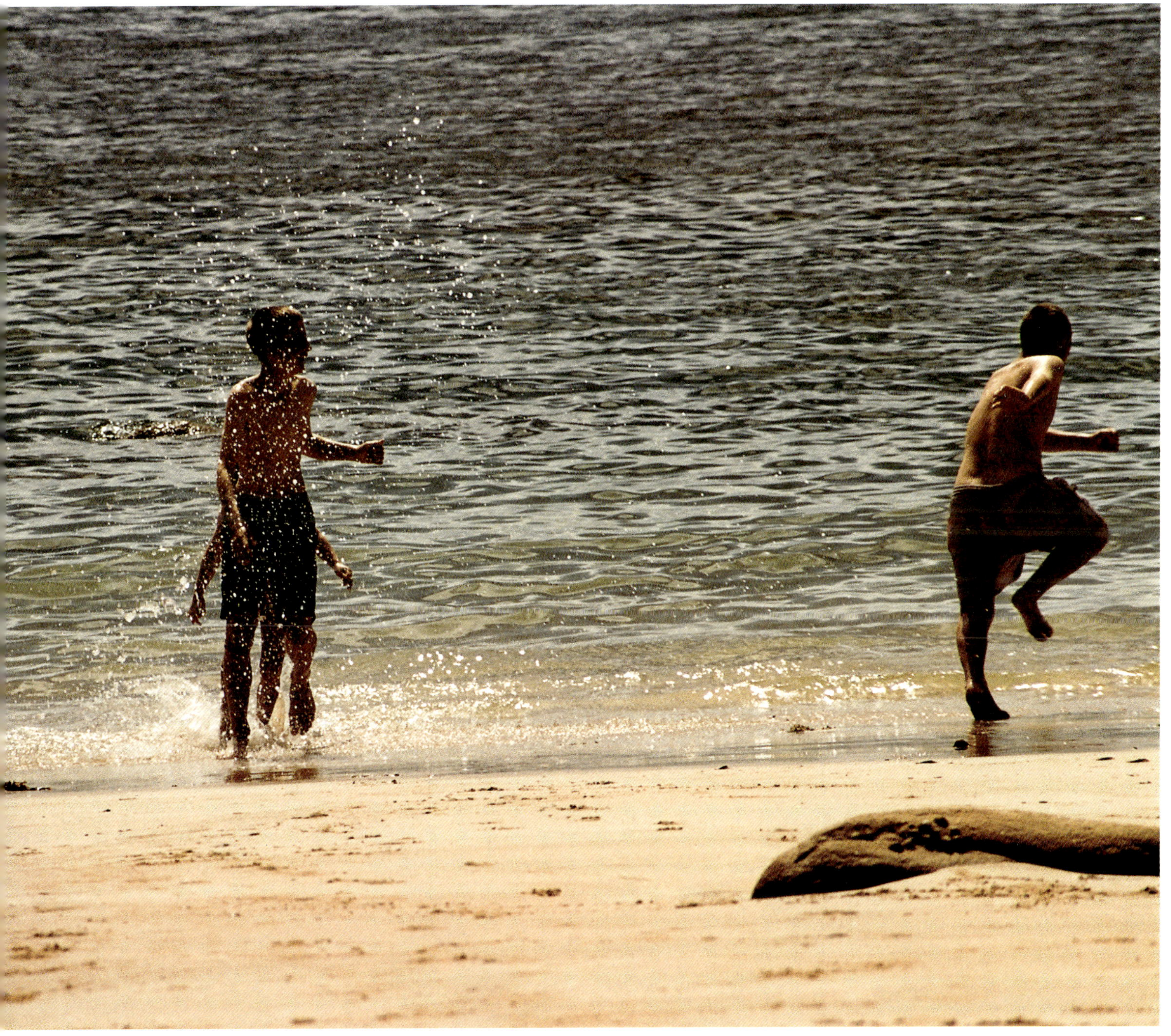

Beauport

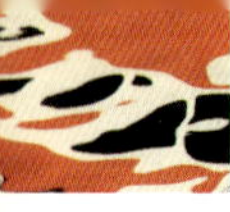

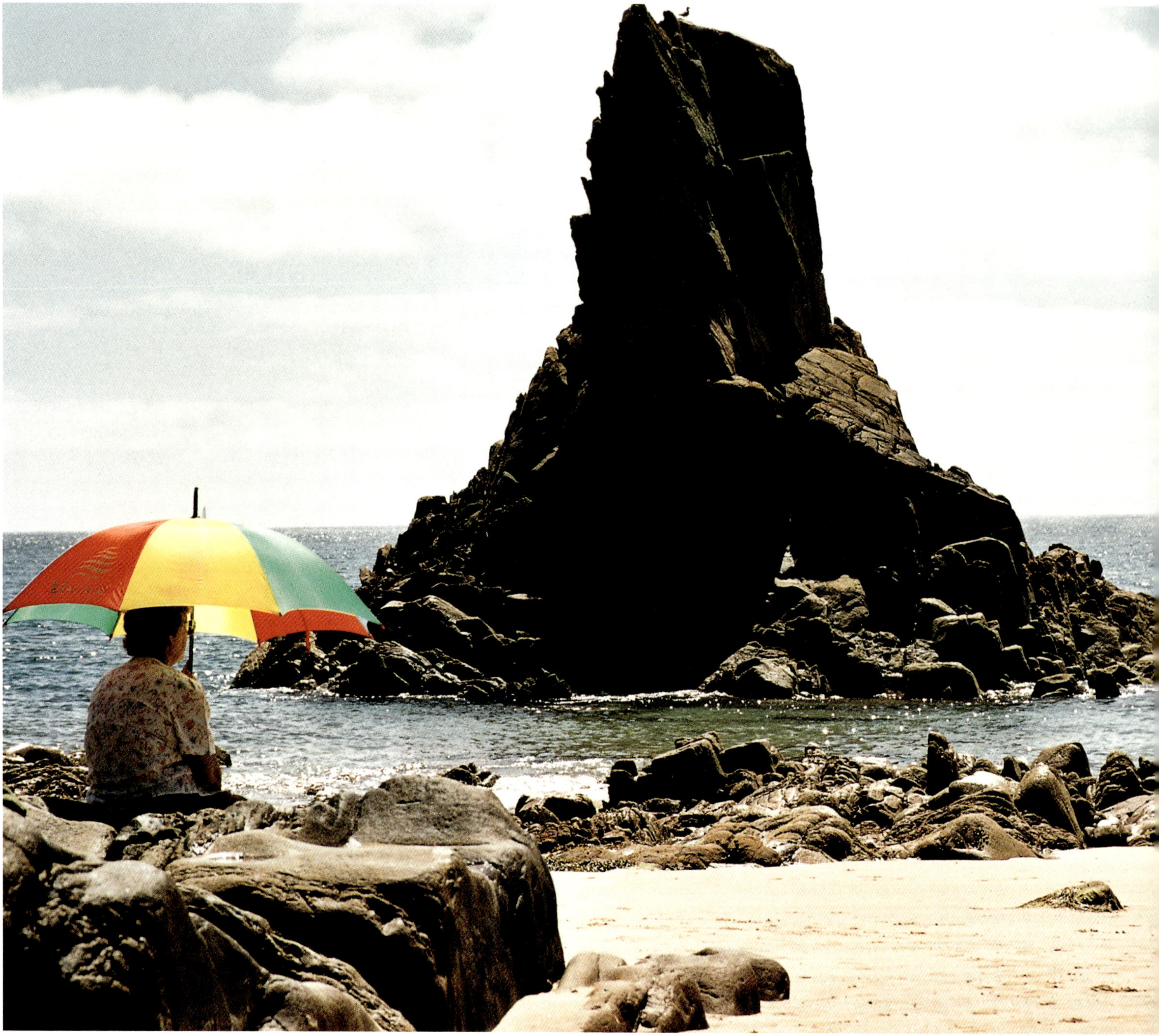

In the Shade, Beauport

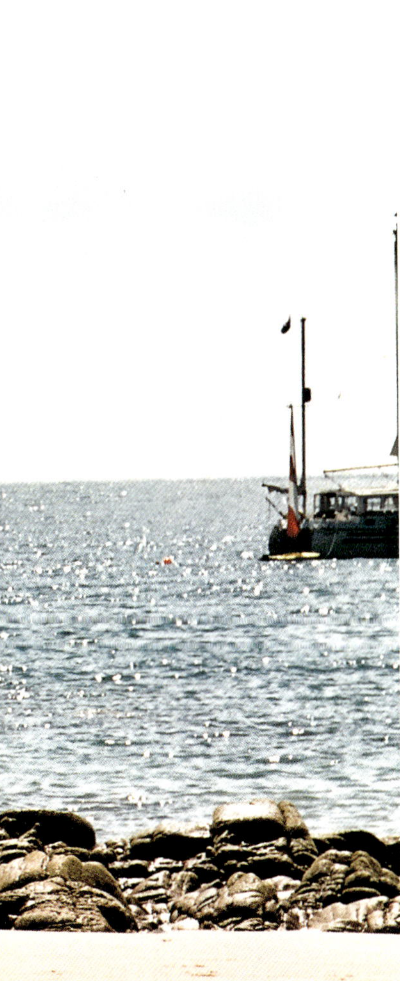

What's She Thinking?

By Lianne Hingston
Les Quennevais

She sits peacefully on the rock.
She stares
Out at the ocean,
What is she thinking?
We don't know.
Is she looking back on her life?
Does she look into her future?
Or is she just enjoying her day out in the sun?
Her umbrella protects her,
Keeping her cool.
She isn't young anymore.
The sun bounces off the rocks
Like a bald man's head
And makes the sea glisten as the lady will listen
As she sits and thinks
And lets the world go by.

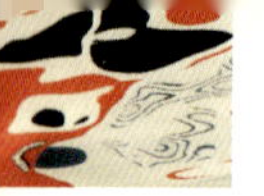

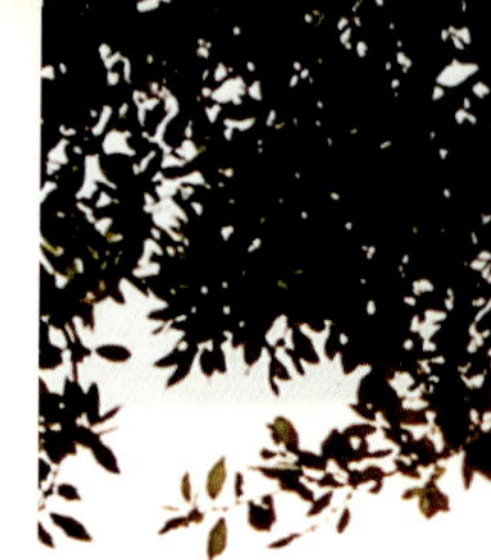

The Sea of Sunshine

By Rebecca Smith

Beaulieu

The dappled sunlight gently touches my face
As I walk down the path to the sand and sea.
I take a deep, clear breath, I can almost taste
The salt on my tongue and the warmth around me.

The path ahead winds down towards the golden sand.
The sea sparkles as the gleaming sun shines.
Waves drift clear and calm until they reach land
Then they break and crash, creating never-ending lines.

The fine sand squeezes between my toes.
I walk slowly, leaving footprints behind.
My identity lost forever, only the sun, sand and sea
Know of my existence, as I contemplate the thoughts
Troubling my mind.

The horizon glistens, the sunlight fades.
The day of sun and fun is over,
My memory lost in the sand and waves.
I'll remember this day for ever...

Janvrin's tomb

By Luke Carney St George's

As the sun awakens, the rays hit my resting place,
And bounce off like young offspring.
The desolate, doleful path leading to my dejected mausoleum,
Which is a crumbling, decayed but proud thing.
The foliage surrounding my bridle-path is like,
A bewildered child making a path in the snow.
Oh, I wish it were those gleeful days when,
Children would dance and swim in my shadow,
But alas, I am condemned to remain on this rock.

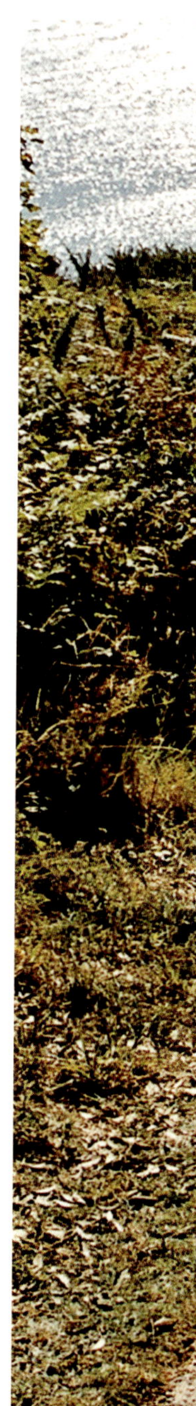

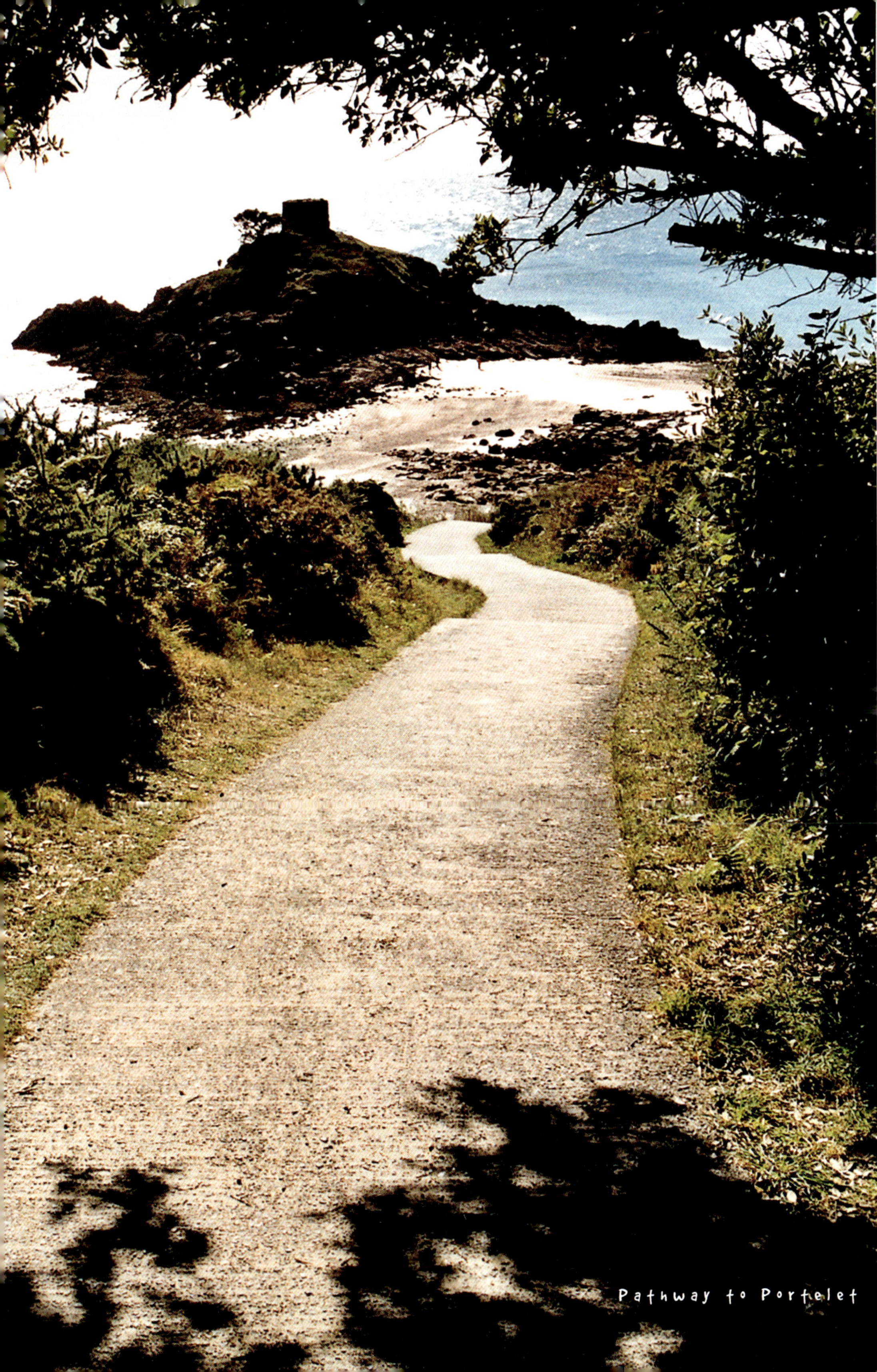

Pathway to Portelet

Path to Peace

By Georgina Graham

St George's

Path to peace,
Leading towards
The silver sea
The golden sand
The sloping island

Path to peace
Passing by
The spiky bushes
The tall trees
The lush green grass

And as you look at this
Glorious view
It seems as though it
Was made for you.

The Depths of the Sea

By Ashley Delgado
Le Rocquier

Raging water at St. Catherine's Breakwater,
I wonder what goes on in the depths.
Maybe there are fish swimming around,
Maybe there are dolphins having fun,
Or maybe there are sharks battling it out.
How I wish I could be a scuba diver,
Then I would explore the sealife,
Swim with the fish,
Play with the dolphins
And battle it out with the sharks.
The sea is a ferocious dog,
But in the depths it is a gentle kitten
It is home to many species,
Who love it dearly, for ever.

White horses and waves,
Rising and falling
The crashing sound, so vibrant,
As seaweed moves with the ebb and flow.

Raging water at St. Catherine's Breakwater,
I wonder what goes on in the depths,
Maybe there are fish swimming around,
Maybe there are dolphins having fun,
Or maybe there are sharks battling it out,
Maybe, I wonder.

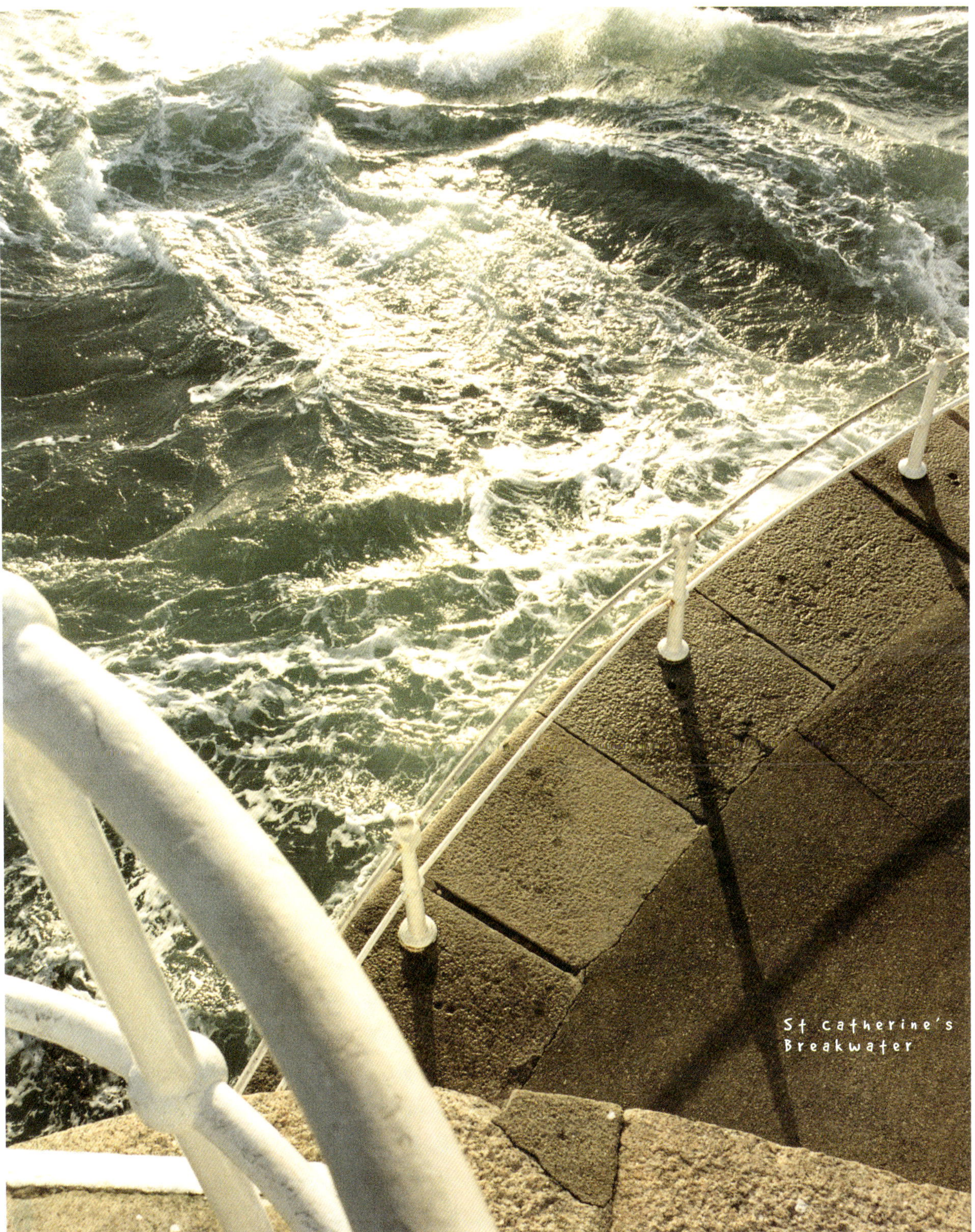
St Catherine's
Breakwater

Poem

By Tom Peters

Victoria College

Ink pots of water glistening like diamonds,
Strewn across the ocean's sand,
A man in the distance fishing alone,
Bag in hand filled with his catch,

Menacing, jagged rocks in the background,
Like the teeth of a crocodile.
Silhouetted beautifully against the sky,
Seymour Tower stands proudly.

The astounding site of this moonlit beach,
Brings sheer joy to my eyes.
This view is one of God's gifts,
Exquisitely arranged to make the ultimate
masterpiece.

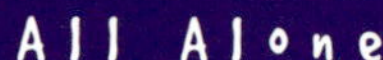

All Alone

By Rachel Dewhurst

Le Rocquier

He only comes down here for peace,
This seeming salty sea dog.
A fisherman, nay, is he.

Each morning he toils and strains in pain,
The bait he digs is for a friend,
For he is a phobic of the sea.

A myriad worms have felt his fork.
Each and every dawning,
Yet a hook he never touches.

The Dawn is his, as even the sea
and sand,
No soul does he see, between he
and land.
This is his private heaven.

The tower is his only friend down here,
Silent but reassuring
All alone is he.

Digging for Bait

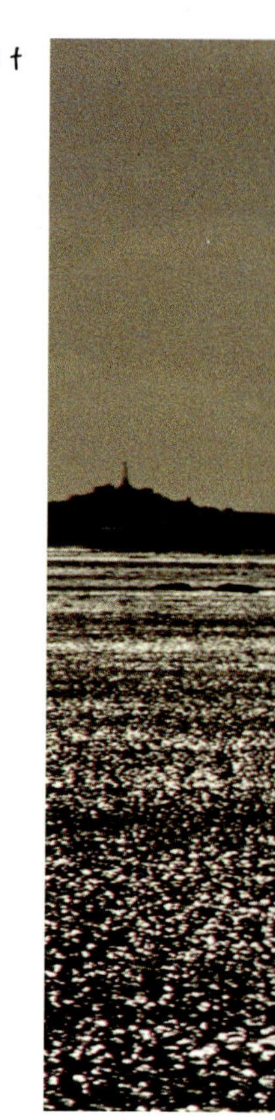

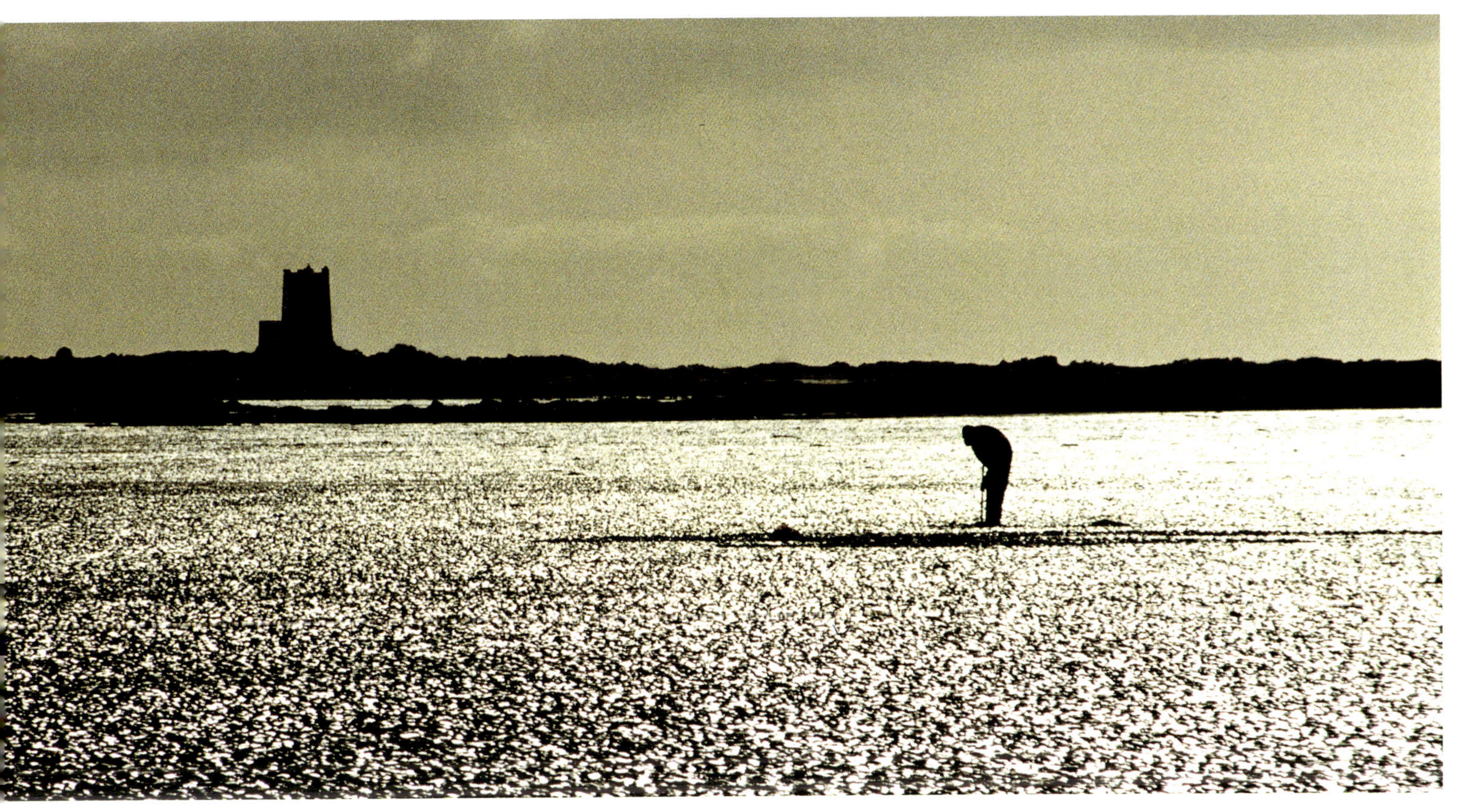

Man, All Alone

By Linda Huet

Le Rocquier

Man, all alone
Early in the morning
Picking bait for his afternoon fishing trip
The wet, winter sand
The cold, wild wind
No one around
Man, all alone.

Man, all alone
Background behind him
Like silhouettes of a castle and roasted rocks
Anyone in the castle?
Anyone, anywhere?
No just the
Man, all alone.

Man, all alone
He needs more bait
He travels further along the sand, leaving
footprints
The wind gets colder
The tide is coming up
He needs to keep warm
Man, all alone.

Man, all alone
He has his bait
He will go home with his bucket
But no one will see
Because he is the
Man, all alone.

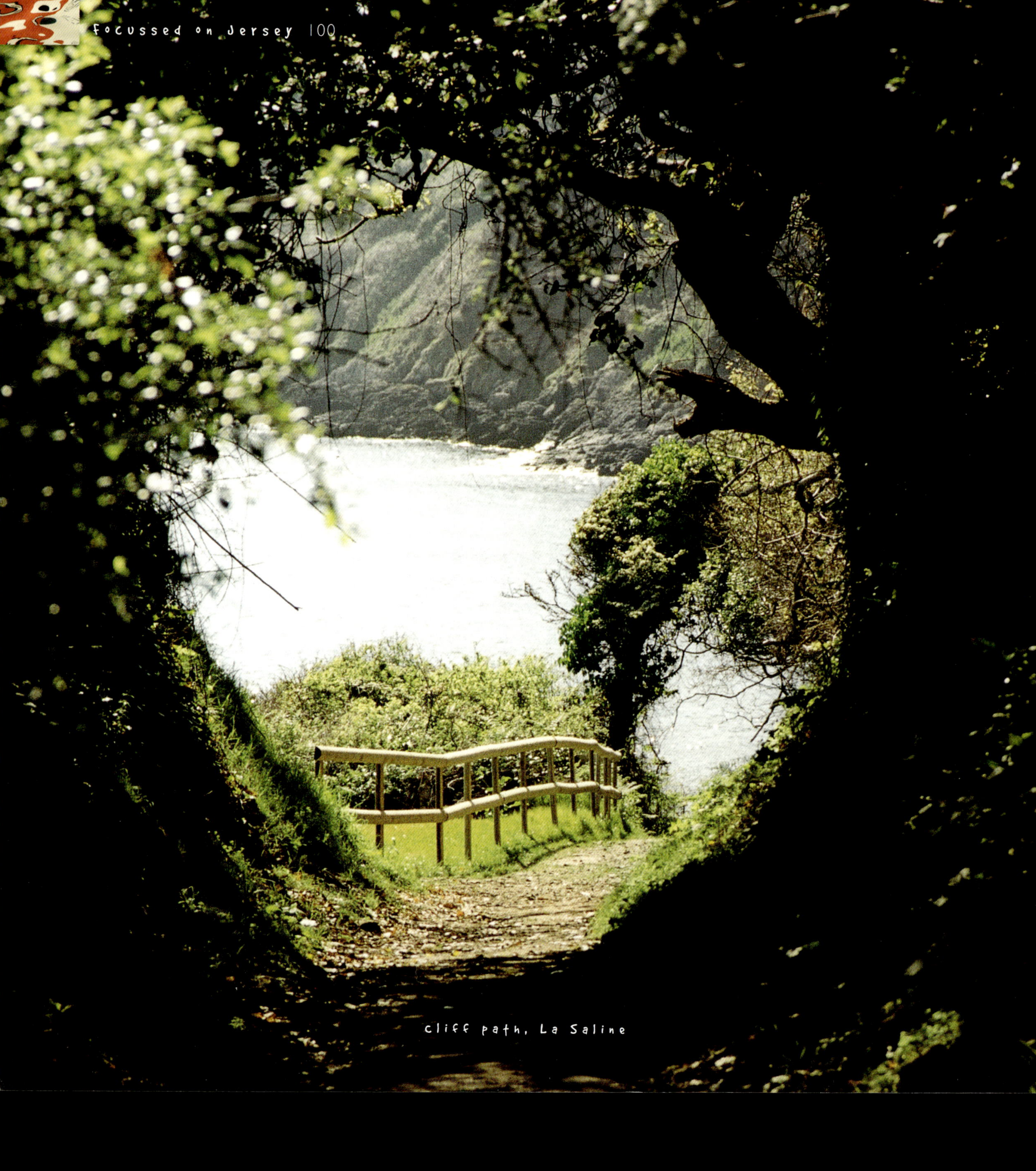

cliff path, La Saline

Spring

By Sally Williams
Grainville

Dappled shadows on the pathway
Light weaving its way through the branches that
form a protective shelter
Scattering patches along the ground.

Leaves line the grassy banks, sloping upwards
Trees which stand tall, rooted firmly in the ground
Occasionally shedding a leaf,
Littering the ground.

Branches joined, making an arch
Through which the lane winds quietly onwards
Gently curving round the corner,
As the path slowly trails off into the distance.

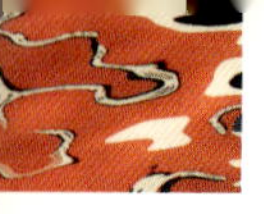

Distant Thoughts

By Alicia Biney
Grainville

My memories are of deep blue seas,
And golden beaches awaiting me,
Of star-swept winds, that beckon me to see
All the wonders calling to me.

I wish I could answer and tell them I'm near,
But even I have a greatest fear,
For family lost, and food I yearn,
Is it too late to take a different turn?

For no one wants me, unwanted and alone,
And it's always the children that cast the first stone,
Memories of hatred cast out those of good,
It seems all my life I've been misunderstood,

Though free that I am, happy I'm not,
Memories of pain, I wish I forgot.
A life without me would be incomplete,
Even though my future seems bleak.

I only wish to withdraw unnoticed,
And to soar through the world undisturbed,
Our worlds would be separate,
But our lives much the same,
Unfortunately for you we'll always remain!

Seagull, La Rocq

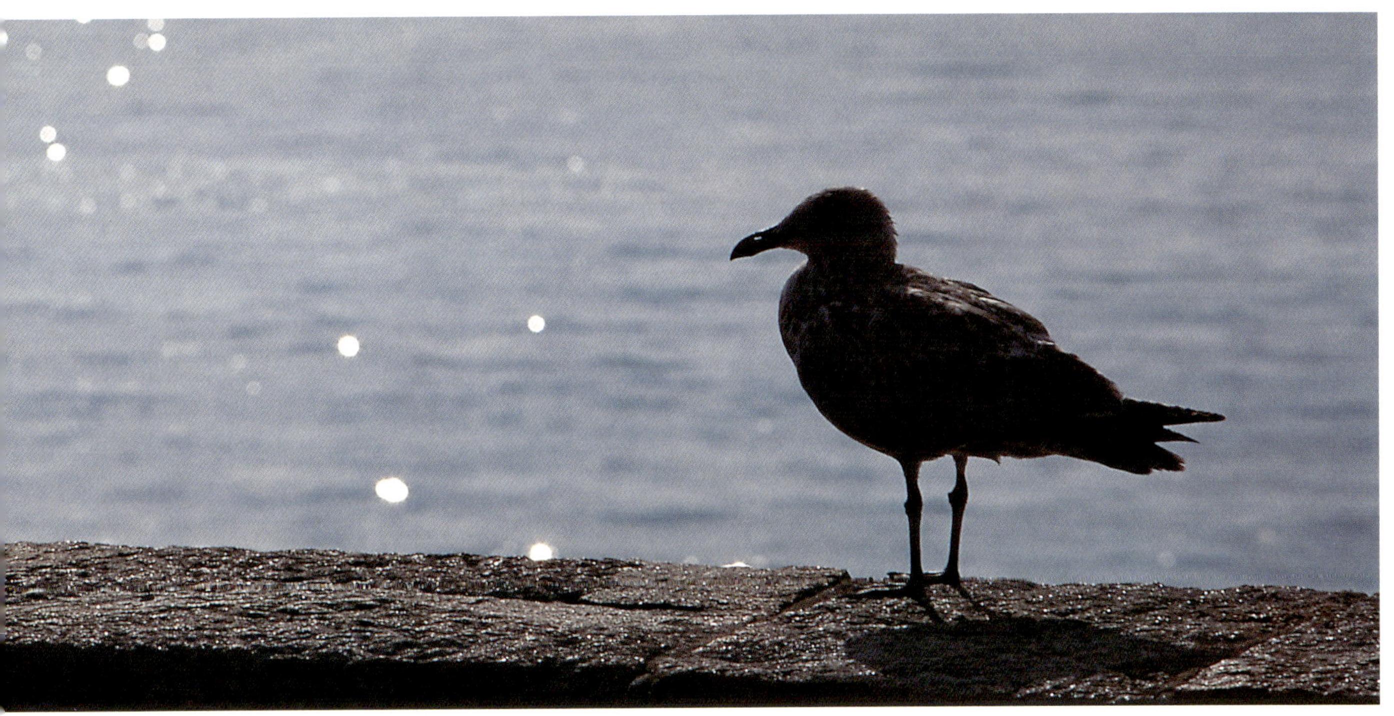

Thoughts of an ageing seagull

By Patrick Cahill
Grainville

As I watch the boats go by.
I think I would rather sail than fly.
Once on the wind I used to soar.
But my old wings can do it no more.

The humans hate me I know that's true.
I would rather be out on the sea so blue.
My savaging ways are not my choice,
I would ask for scraps if I had a voice.

From behind the boat I used to get my fish.
Now it's from the bins, I get my dish.
I love to swoop and bob on the sea,
But now time is catching up with me.

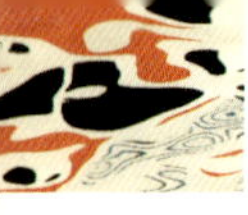

The Waterfall

By Nick Harvey
De La Salle

The water flows,
Sending peace and tranquility,
Cleansing our souls of the yearly sins.
The water flows
Flows,
Flows
And flows,
Filling our souls.

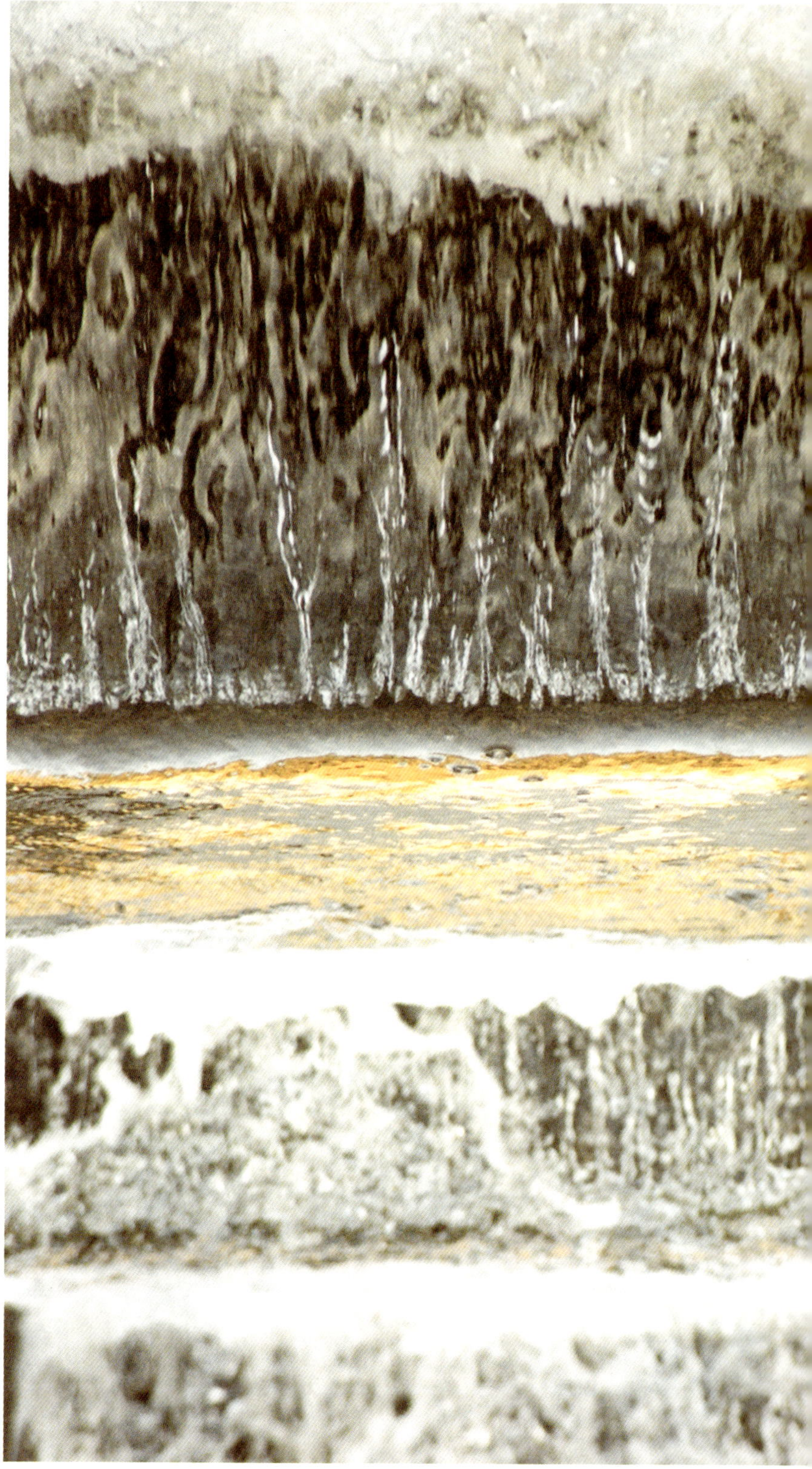

Valle des Vaux

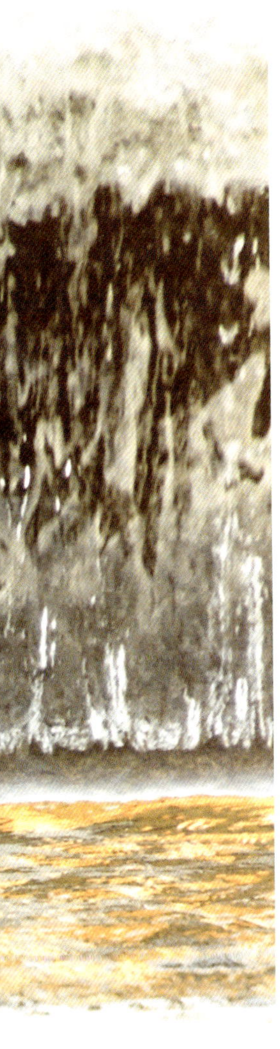

Jersey waterfall

By Stephanie Anderson
Hautlieu

A confused, blurring mess,
My mind, life and soul.
Empty and awash just like the
merging water at the top of a waterfall.

The sound of dripping water runs through me.
Depressed and lonely I think about the
refreshing, calm place I love the most.
Weakness laps at my mind - and spills.

The confusion begins to fade as I think
about the tranquil golden pool.
My mind fills with rich thoughts
about these steps of pure goodness.

The crystal-clear chandelier gems
fall to create a small delicate
splash in the foamy waters below,
The colour of ice.

Higher, higher the foam jewels
rise, singing my happiness and joy,
Through the clear
Jersey waters.

At The End of the Day

By Lizzie Pocock
Jersey College for Girls

The tower commands a tranquil scene.
Across the sun-speckled bay,
The solitary boats are left alone to muse
Upon thoughts from the tiring day.

From raging winds and threatening seas
The boats at last return
To the sound of gently lapping waves
And a watchful eye of concern.

For the tower, it seems, has a fatherly air
And will not rest until all are home;
And then, contented, will sleep at last,
Whilst the moon takes watch, alone.

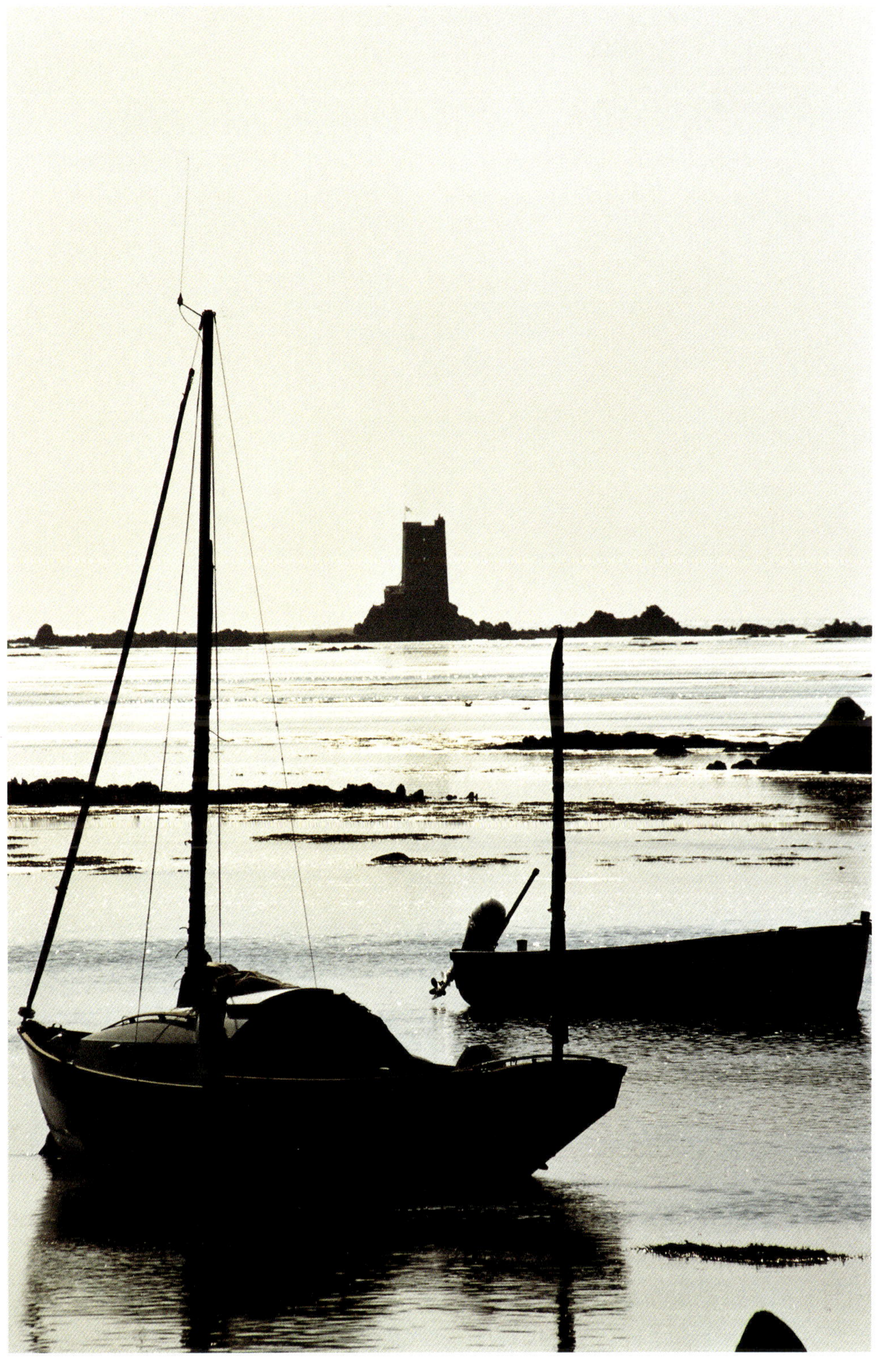

View from
Green Island

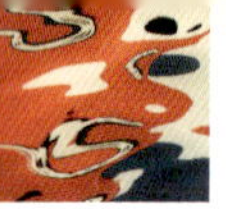

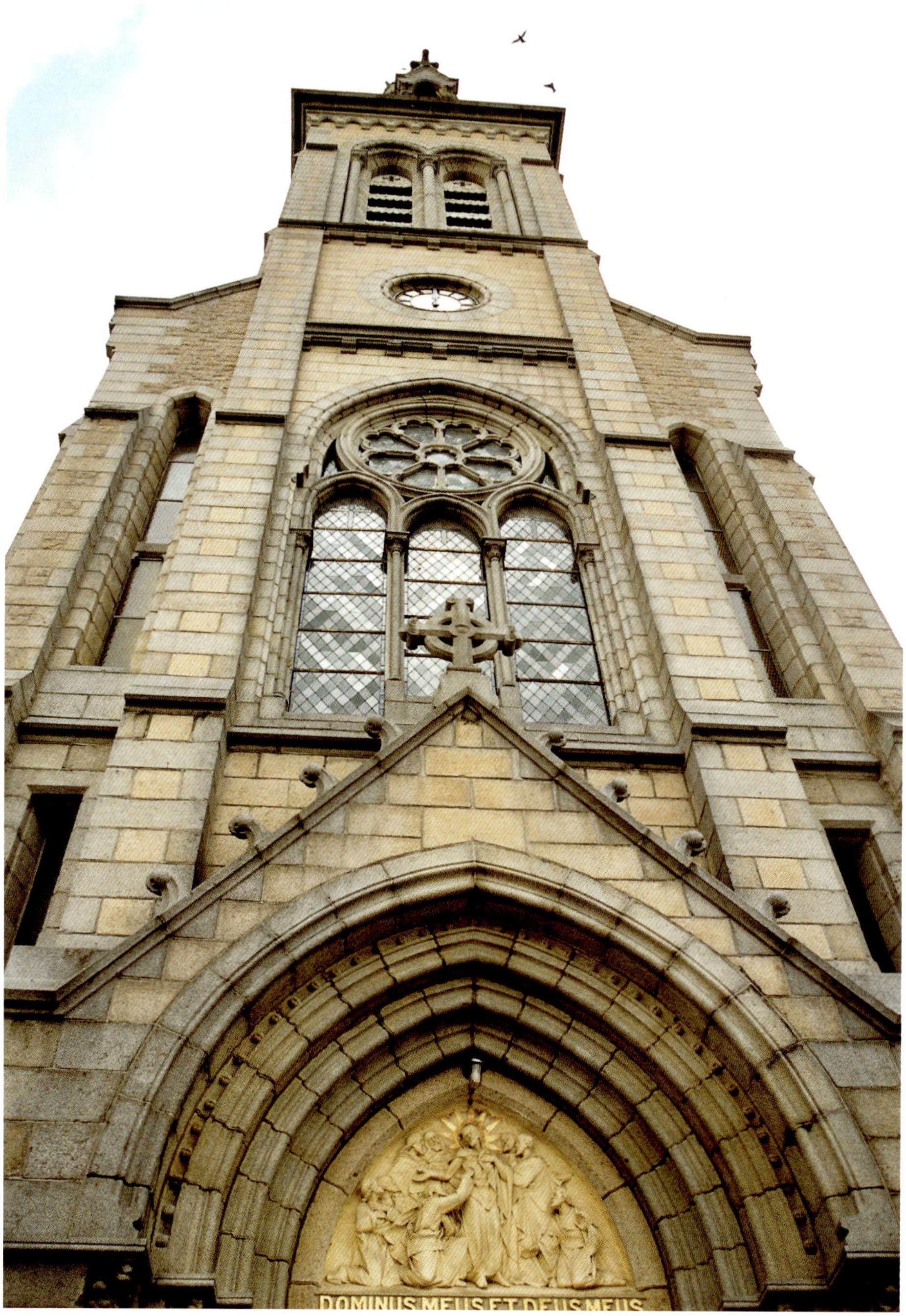

St Thomas church

Butterflies

By Megan Davies
Beaulieu

Standing outside this grand building,
Bells ringing, echoing inside my head.
Today is meant to be the happiest
of my life.

Yet I feel nothing, no joy,
no excitement, not even nervous.
just numb.

Laughter of a happy couple
drifts by, and suddenly an
explosion of butterflies flutter
randomly somewhere deep inside me.
My palms are sweaty,
a flood of anticipation flows
through my veins.

My mind is full of colour,
a sea of images, this
House of God stands before me.

And now as I enter this
Magnificent structure
I have only one thought,
It is my turn to walk up the aisle.

BEL-VAL
ROYALS!
Sweet Peas 50p
Courgettes 50p per bag
Rhubarb 50p
JERSEY ROYAL POTATOES
LIC. No. 51
PINKS 40p
Anemones 50p

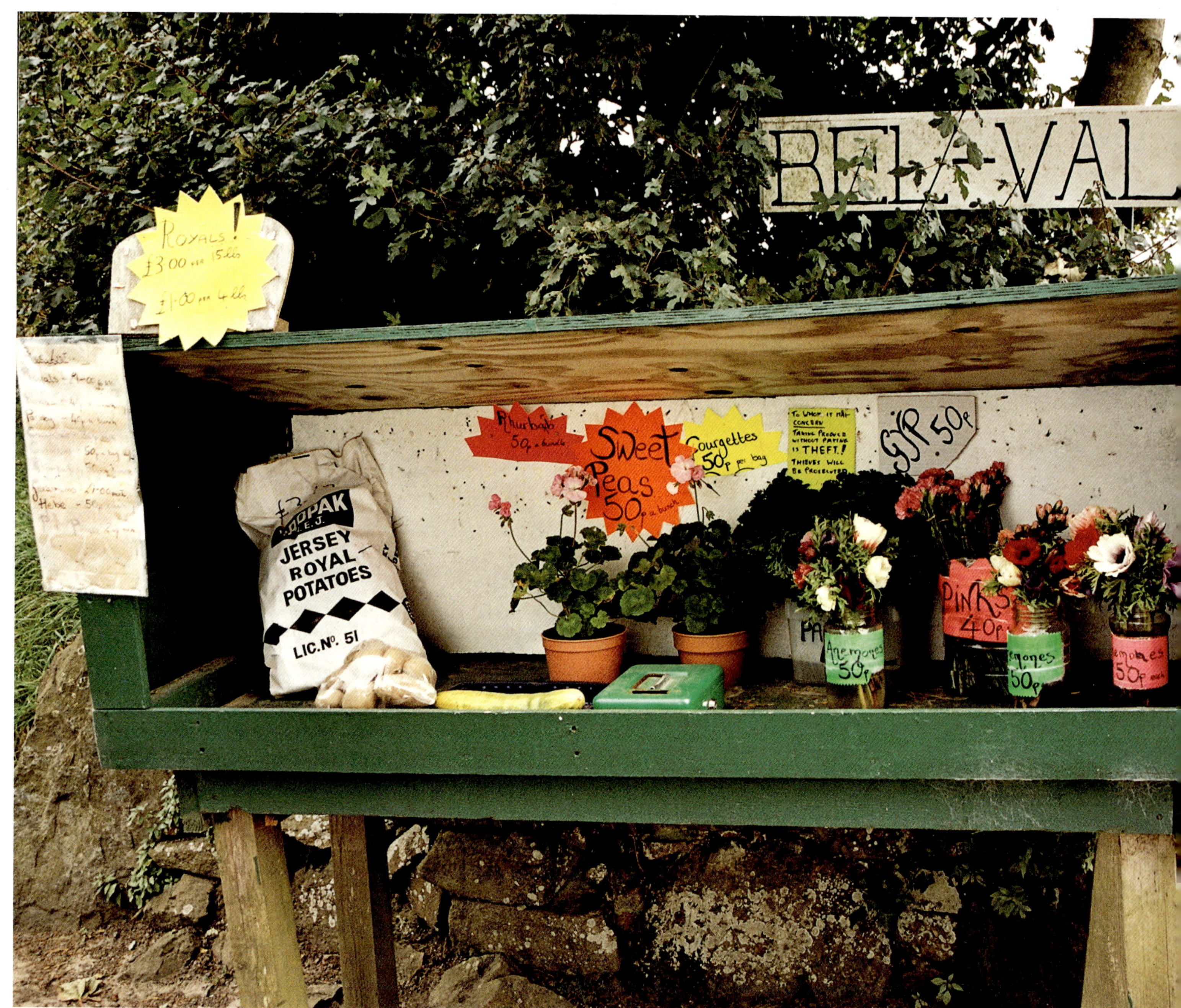

Bel Val

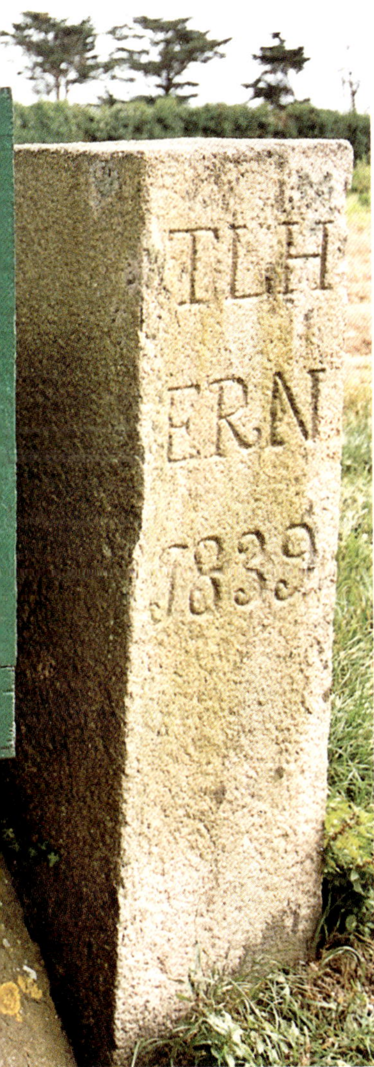

Time

By Stephen Prosser

Hautlieu

Tranquil country lanes,
Lead to a lone farmstead,
Its ancient granite walls,
Watch the travellers on the road,
Horses, carts, bikes and cars,
Trapped in a timeline of its own.

Outside the house a wooden box stands,
Offering its goods to a weary customer,
Rhubarb, sweet peas
Courgettes, Jersey Royals,
And pretty pink flowers.
Put your shilling in the box,
Put your pound in the box,
Its seen them all.

A once common site in the lanes of Jersey,
Now not so common,
Like a dying species,
Traditional Jersey slowly fading,
Slowly fading,
Fading.

Summer Memories

By Lisa Davy

Le Rocquier

Children playing in the sea,
Something that I long to see.
Children playing in the sand,
Running about hand in hand.

People lying on the beach,
While water comes to touch their feet.
People swimming like the fish,
But, they're gone with a swish.

The sun glittering on the waves,
The rocks go round like a big maze.
The beautiful yacht across the bay,
When I looked it turned my way.

The magic clouds in the sky,
All the colours I see in my eye.
Greys and blues and whites I see,
Go together with the glistening sea.

Summer memories are for me,
Of sandy beach and ice cold sea.
Of shells and pebbles on the shore
Of ice-cream, rock and so much more.

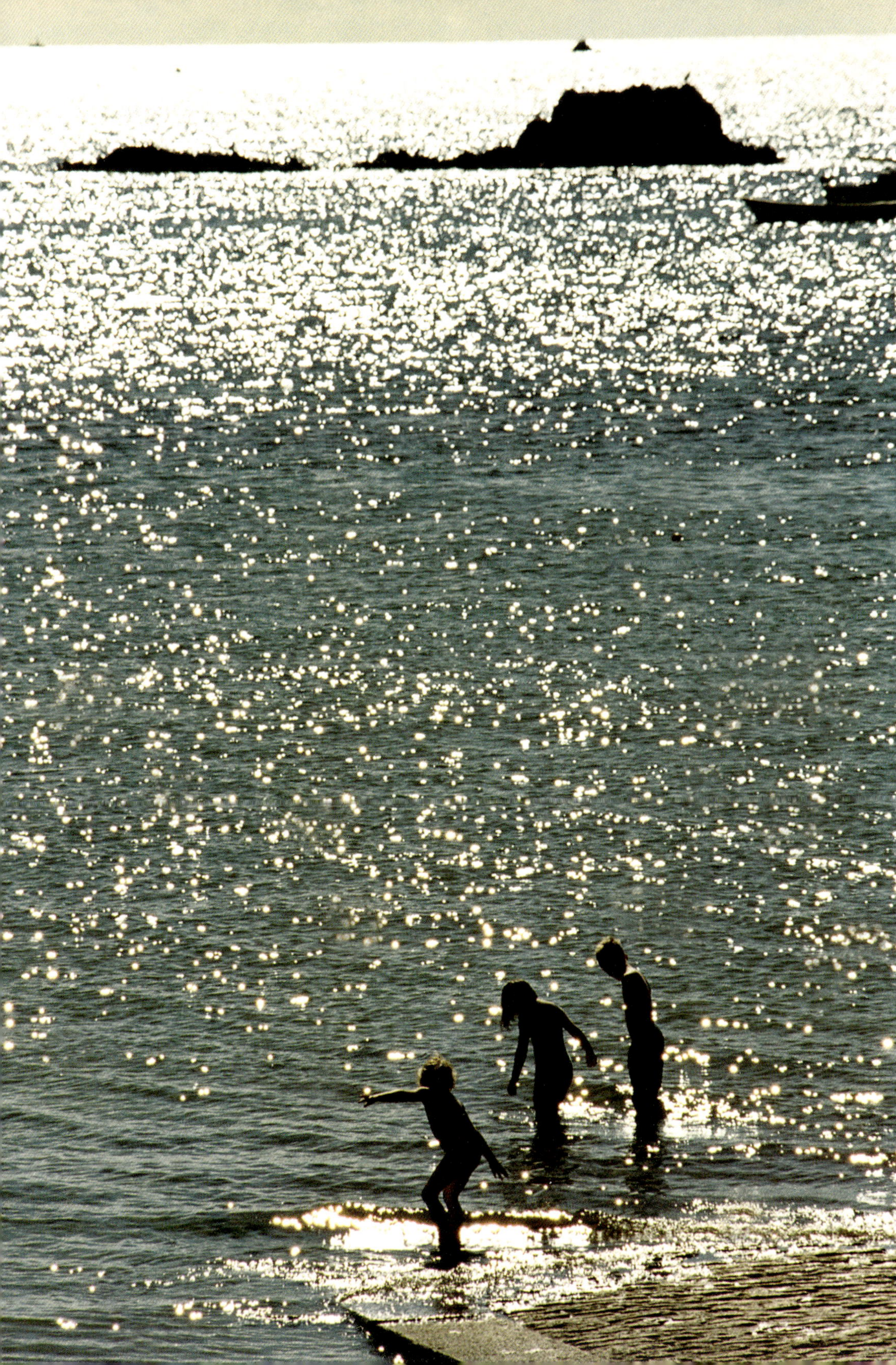

Le Rocque

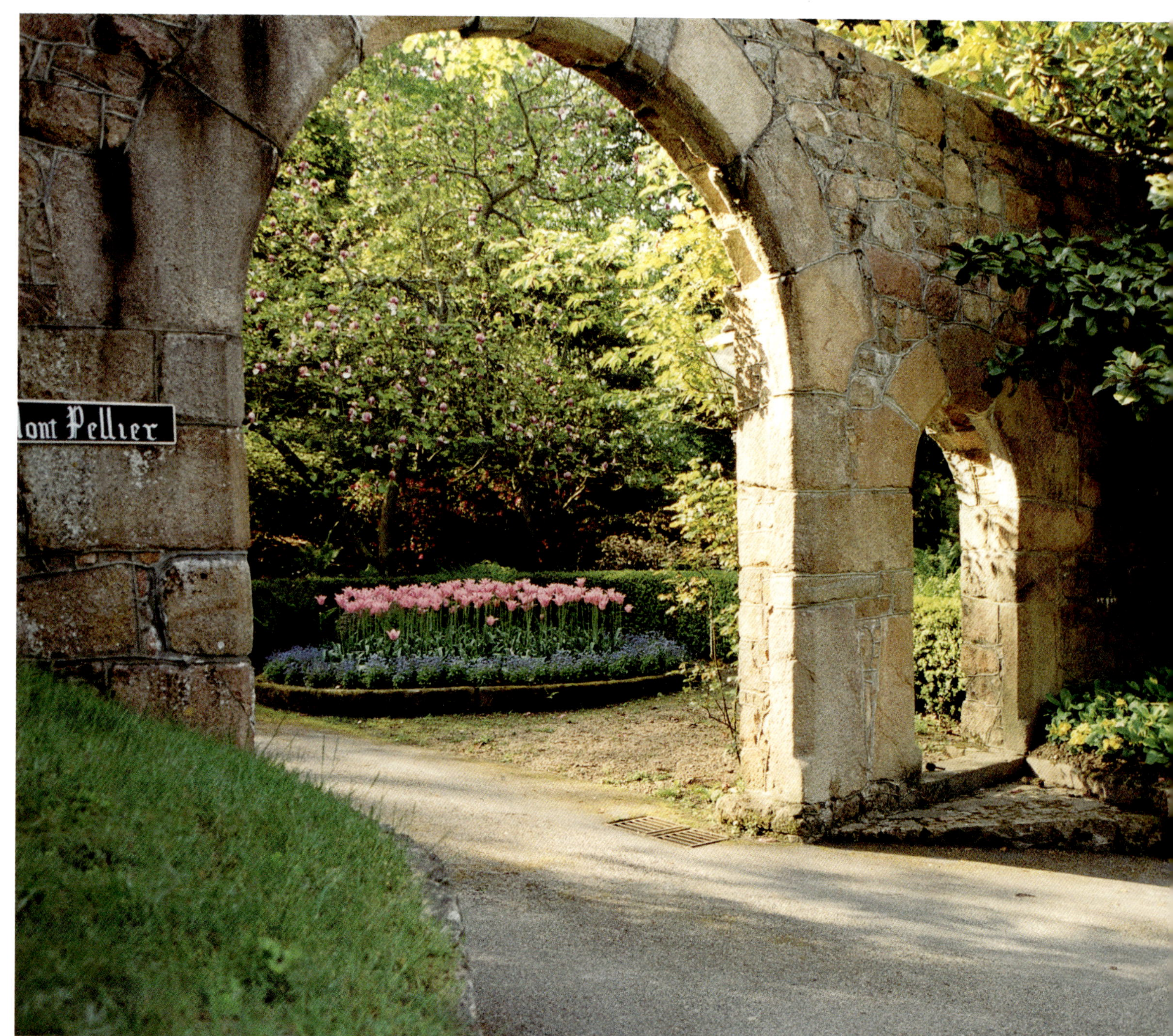

Montpellier

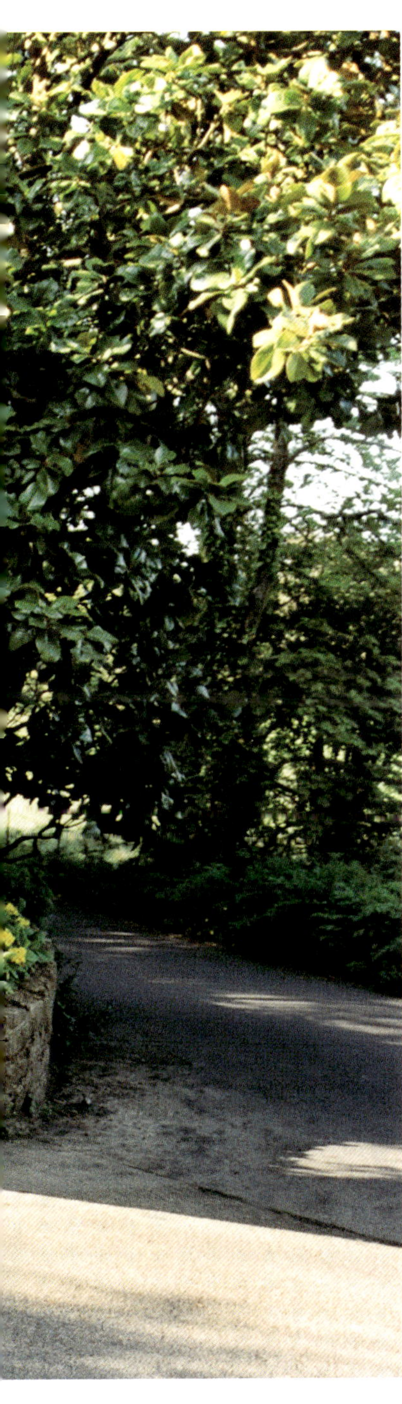

What lies through the archway?

By Jennie Crocker
Les Quennevais

What lies through the archway?
Where the sun shines bright and hot,
Where the trees are the only shade,
And the driveway's made of rock.

It looks like such a happy place,
Among the many flowers.
A scene from a fairytale,
Of a princess in a tower

What lies through the archway?
Should I take a look?
Is it hiding a country lane?
Or a babbling brook?

Does it hold a well-kept secret?
Of love or even sorrow.
What lies through the archway?
Maybe I'll find out tomorrow.

Here I stand

By Josh O'Brien
Grainville

Here I stand, alone with only the sea around
Just me and the little shoots of grass.

Now it's cold, and damp wintertime, I think,
No one ever comes to visit me.

Now I've stood here years and still I stand tall
And yet I haven't moved a bit, not slightly, not at all.

The waves still hit me as hard as they possibly can
But no, I'm still standing here and still I wear the crown.

Now I'm getting bored of this loneliness, and the benches always bare
Will they ever knock me down? To be honest I don't care.

But once, just once, I'd like to see
These waves show some respect for me.

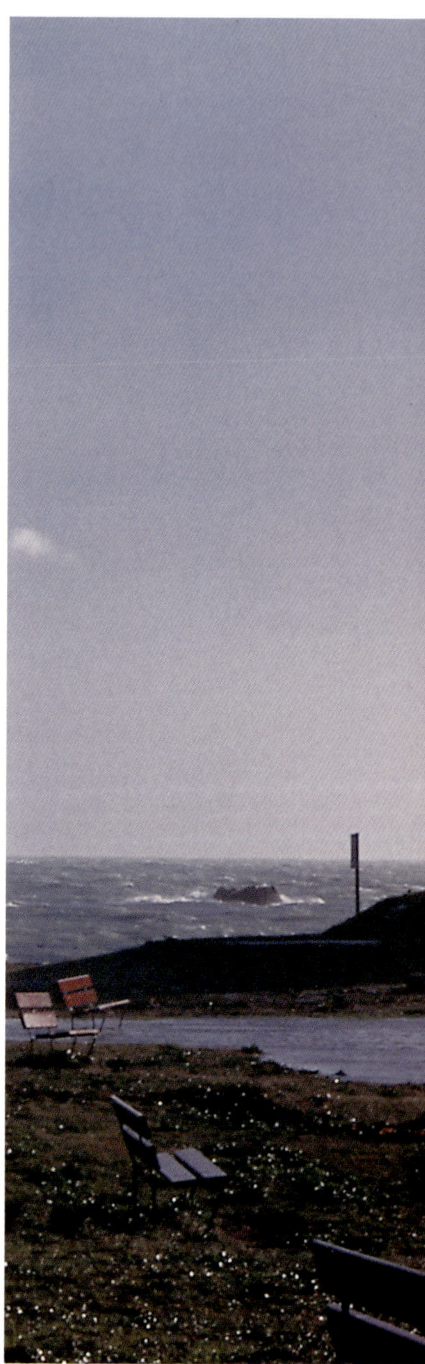

Waves at Le Hocq

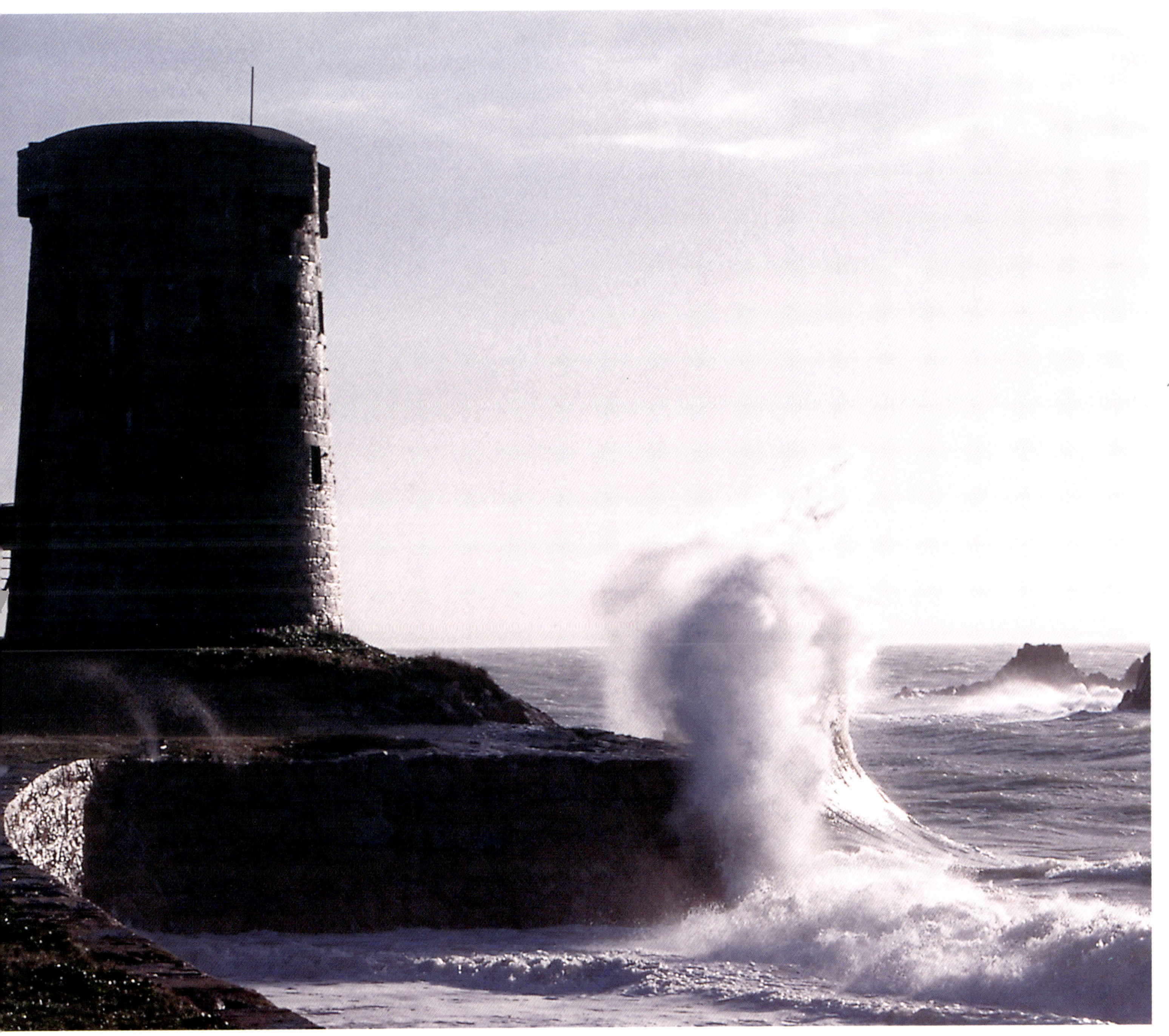

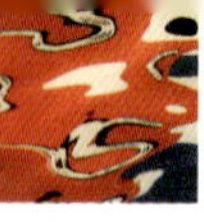

Defying Water

By Paul Ahier

Granville

I stand, defying water,
The waves lap against my sides,
The fisherman on my back,
The tourists pace up and down,
Wearing down my spine,
Standing, defying water.

I stand, defying water,
The sun is going down,
Everyone goes home
As clouds loom overhead,
Till tomorrow they come again,
The cold bites at the stone that lines my sides.

I stand, defying water,
The guardian of boats floating in the bay.
A storm is brewing, but all is calm,
The night draws in,
Standing, defying water
ALONE.

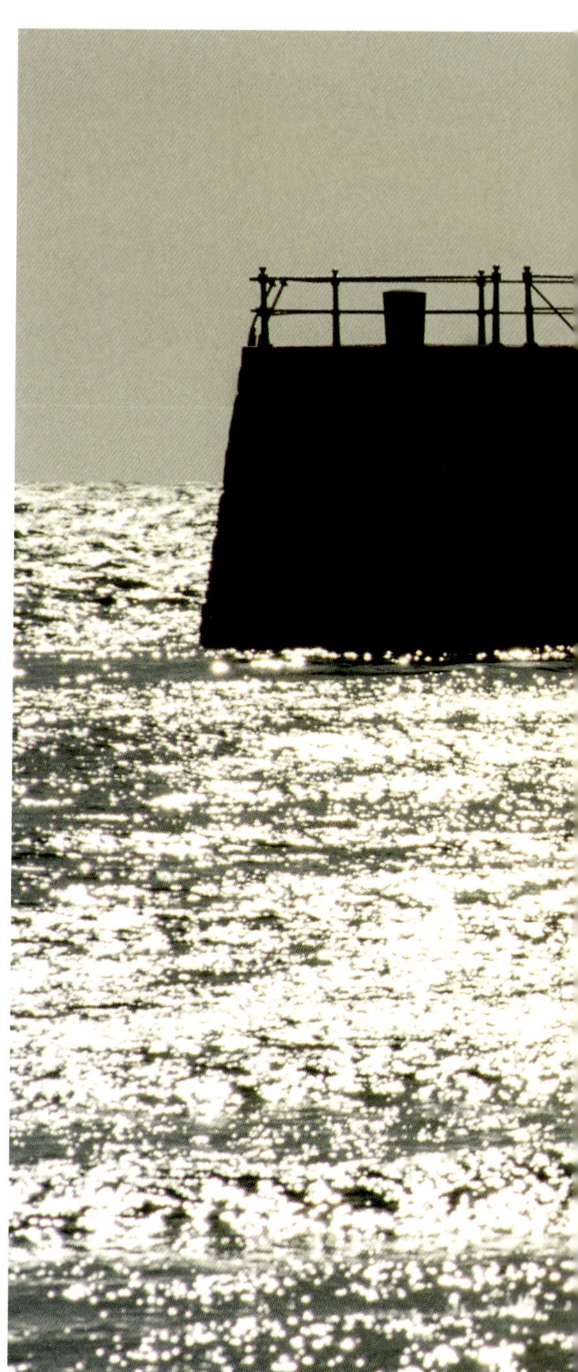

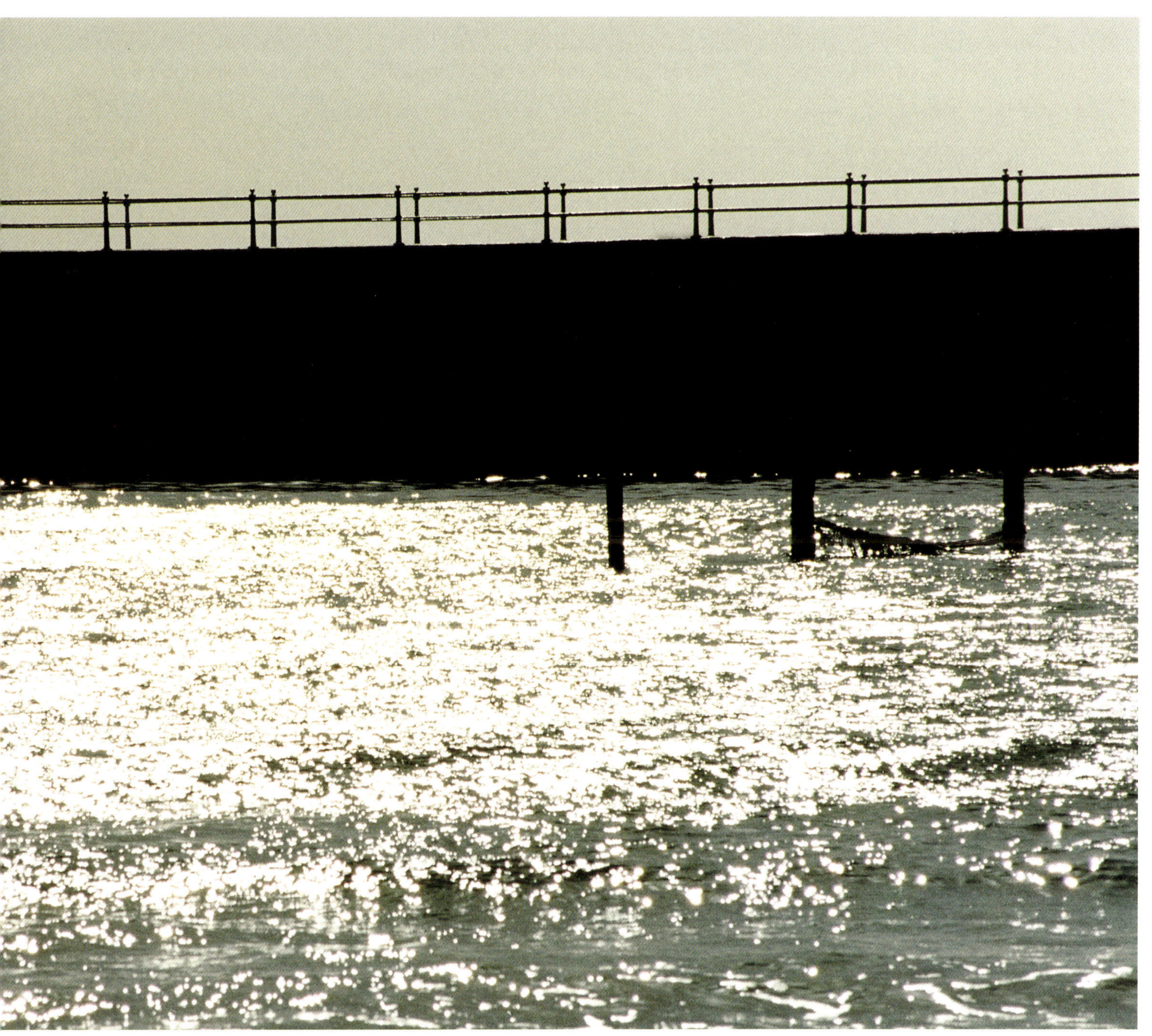

St Brelade's Pier

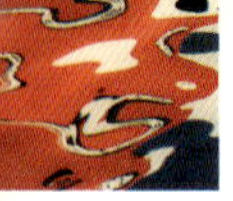

Mooring Posts, Le Hocq

The Tragedy of My Heart And Soul

By Heidi Heslop

Haute Valleé

My heart insatiable, unappeasable,
Only she may quench my aspiration,
My hunger, my eternal passion,
Only she can grant my dream, my true purpose.

I long to feel the freshness of the incessant sea,
I yearn to experience once more her beauty,
The refinement of her touch,
To have her grace my presence once more.

I close my eyes and consider,
I reflect on our last meeting,
How all those years ago she stole my heart
And has never brought it back.

Oh how I listen every night,
I know she pities my existence,
But her wishes unfamiliar,
So unknown to me.

What am I but lowly timber?
Too unrefined and crude to be important,
She enlightens me but every night
Of how I signify so much.

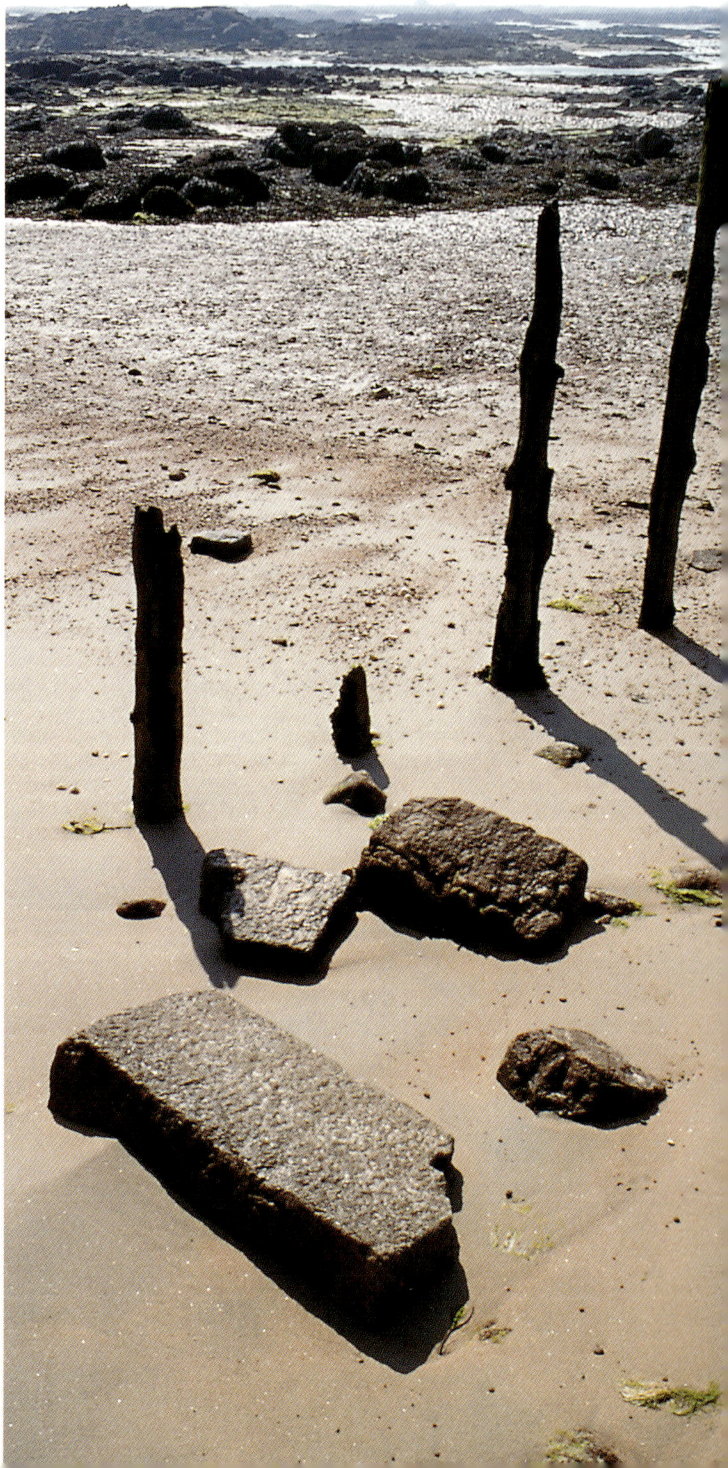

But all I signify is the pain of this world,
I show the suffering in my weathered arms,
Tender aching in my arching spine,
Cruelty in my wasted stumps.

Twice a day she does go
And twice a day she revisits,
I believe she loves me like a son,
Why after all, she's always been here.

From my birth when I was planted,
Immaculate with sheen and arrogant
with splendour,
She did but warn me of my fate,
Urged me to accept my rank, just a
mooring, just kindling.

But I was so much more than that,
I was youthful and liberated,
Nothing in the vast world could possibly
hold me back,
Not me.

I now look out to my love
And await her placid visit,
She has long forgiven the error of my ways
But not before my punishment.

My purpose to begin with was to stand strong,
Do what no man could and withstand the tide,
Defend the precocious boat
That I held anchored.

But she, she had different plans,
Whipped up a storm so bad the boat
broke lose,
It sailed away to its death,
Smashing into a million pieces on the rocks.

She was so burly and potent,
She tore me to shreds; I'm now but a shrine
To my former existence.

I now gaze upon the sun-kissed sands,
Listen as the sea drifts high above my head,
Feel the whole beach beneath my toes,
Taste the beauty and wisdom of the sea.

For she is endless
And with time grows more magnificent,
I will only rot and
Deteriorate with time.

No one will remember me,
No one will care when I'm gone,
My life strewn in between the waves,
My thoughts drifting with the breeze.

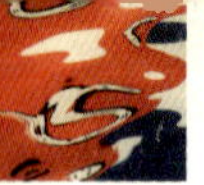

contributors

Acknowledgements.

The Cobwebs of this ageing mind have been blown skywards by the Students involved in this undertaking. If I have created the stimulus for the ambience of this book then I am a very proud person.

I would like to thank Mario Lundy and Pat Allen of Grainville School, who were the initial people who gave me the space to air my thoughts, and through this my idea developed.

All of the teachers in the schools were incredible in the way they accepted this 'strange individual' into their environment and helped create this project.

Big thanks to Tom McKeon and Len Norman who told me to 'get on with it!'

To Wendy Hurford, MBE who guided us through the difficult choice of it all.

To my wife, Dezi, who guided my confused brain through this project. To my Mum and family who all support me in their different ways.

To Martyn Farley and his team for all their time, patience and expertise.

But the Biggest Thanks to all the Students who helped to produce this with their Amazing Enthusiasm.

So many Thank - You's!
Maybe Volume two?..

Brian Skelley.